explorations
in
LANGUAGE

To the Master and Fellows of
Selwyn College, in gratitude for their
hospitality and encouragement.

explorations
in
LANGUAGE

A. J. Tinkel

CAMBRIDGE
UNIVERSITY PRESS

Published by the Press Syndicate of the University of Cambridge
The Pitt Building, Trumpington Street, Cambridge CB2 1RP
40 West 20th Street, New York, NY 10011–4211, USA
10 Stamford Road, Oakleigh, Melbourne 3166, Australia

First published 1988
Fourth printing 1993

Printed in Great Britain at the University Press, Cambridge

British Library cataloguing in publication data

Tinkel, A. J.
Explorations in Language.
1. English language
I. Title
420   PE1072

Library of Congress cataloguing in publication data

Explorations in language / A. J. Tinkel.
1. Language and languages.   I. Title.
P106   T498   1988

ISBN 0 521 33606 6

CE

The photograph on p. 7 (top left) is from the Central television
production *Birth of a Nation*, reproduced by permission of
Central Independent Television plc.

All other photographs are by David Runnacles.

Contents

Contents

Foreword
by J. L. M. Trim

It is a great pleasure for me to be asked to contribute a brief foreword to Anthony Tinkel's *Explorations in Language*. As an academic phonetician and linguist I have always been convinced that the growth of language skills should go hand-in-hand with an awareness of the workings of language within us and in our environment. I feel the absence of any systematic promotion of language awareness in our educational provision to be responsible for the ignorance and prejudice which characterise most public discussions of language issues and which have vitiated successive attempts to produce sensible language policies in public life and education.

Some thirty years ago, I set down some thoughts on speech education as a contribution to Smith and Quirk's *The Teaching of English*: suggesting its aim should be 'to evolve an approach to speech work from a coherent developing body of knowledge concerning the nature of spoken language and its role in human affairs. Not only must the teacher work from such a background, but the pupil too should have the sense of a developing linguistic whole, in which special knowledge and special skills are integrated. It is because our spoken language is the matrix of our experience, which it unifies and structures, that I regard the totality of work in spoken language as a humanizing experience deserving the name of an education.' It was clear to me that in order to bring about educational change, academics must establish a partnership with the teachers, who are most closely in touch with the way in which young minds work and develop. It is, furthermore, the classroom teacher who is in a position to observe the learners' reaction to materials and methods so as to develop and adapt them over a period of time. It was therefore most welcome when Anthony Tinkel, as a practising teacher, having taken an M.A. in Applied Linguistics in the University of Essex, spent a further year working for the Cambridge M.Phil. Theoretical Linguistics under my supervision and chose for his dissertation topic a justified syllabus for a course in basic linguistics at advanced level.

Since that time, Anthony Tinkel has spent more than a decade patiently developing and refining a course and supporting materials, trying them out in different schools and moving cautiously and steadily to establish the practical basis for an examinable subject at advanced level. It has been a source of considerable personal satisfaction to me in recent years to be privileged to pay an annual visit to The Oratory School at Woodcote to follow the development and to make a modest contribution to the course by giving a lesson, with the approval of a supportive and forward-looking headmaster.

This is perhaps also the place to acknowledge the encouragement given to the 'language awareness' movement by the National Congress of Language in Education, particularly by Eric Hawkins, John Sinclair and Gillian Donmall, and by Cambridge University Press as publishers both of the present volume and of the series edited by Professor Hawkins.

I am glad that Anthony Tinkel has taken such care to develop and so frequently revise his text, and to adopt the basic 'exploratory' approach. The effect is to reduce to an inescapable minimum the conveying of facts and to lead the young person through a voyage of discovery, raising to conscious awareness the tacit mastery of language, that extraordinary complex mental instrument we are able to call upon and bring into immediate action for all the multifarious purposes of our daily lives, in their practical, intellectual and emotional aspects. The value of that awareness for careers of all kinds, in a society which demands ever greater communication skills from its members, is immense. Anthony Tinkel's careful and stimulating guidance will help teachers and pupils alike to make the voyage of linguistic self-discovery with profit and pleasure.

Acknowledgements

The trail that leads to the appearance of this book goes back seventeen years. During that time many people have helped me and their names cry out for mention. If I have omitted to mention anyone whose name does belong here, I hope I shall be forgiven.

It was during a year spent at the University of Essex in 1970–71 that I first began to consider how the study of language might be more effectively presented to older secondary school pupils and those embarking on language courses in higher education. I received much encouragement to pursue this idea, then and later, from the Head of the Language Centre, Professor Peter Strevens, and from Dr Terry Moore, now of the Department of Linguistics at the University of Cambridge. I am also very aware that I would never have been able to spend that year at the University of Essex without the active initiative of John Kendall-Carpenter, my headmaster of the time at Cranbrook School, Kent.

Three years later, as I embarked on a further year's post-graduate study in the Department of Linguistics at the University of Cambridge, I had the great good fortune to meet Dr John Trim, then Director of the Department. Since that date John Trim has been an inexhaustible source of advice and warning, encouragement and guidance, without which this book would not have been written. Whatever the reader finds to admire within this book will almost certainly be attributable to John Trim's influence.

The writing of the book began during a term's Schoolmaster Fellowship at Selwyn College, Cambridge. I shall always be in the debt of the then Master, Sir Owen Chadwick, and the Fellows of the College for putting their faith in an untried educational project. Their interest and positive encouragement has continued uninterrupted since my term among them and has helped to sustain me through difficult periods of the writing.

I am conscious that I would not have been able to take up my Fellowship without the active efforts of Mrs C. A. Huggins, my head of the time at Southlands Girls School, Reading. I am indebted to her and also to my colleagues in the Modern Languages Department – Mrs Irene Allan, Mrs Jay Davies and Mrs Vera Jobson – for their support and encouragement at that time.

Since rejoining the staff of The Oratory School I have received unstinted support of all kinds from the headmaster, Adrian Snow. Through his actions I have been relieved of many of the worries that face the author as he prepares a manuscript for the publisher. He has also given me the chance to test and develop ideas in practice. My colleagues on The Oratory's staff have shown me unabated interest and kindness, as publication has approached. I hope they will not take it amiss if I only mention for particular thanks Mrs Alison Harris, Andrew Nash and Mairi and Tom McIntyre, who have given of their valuable time to provide me with informed and considered reaction to the manuscript.

I am grateful to Howard King, Secretary of the Oxford and Cambridge Schools Examination Board, and to George Wiley, one of its Chief Examiners, for enabling the AO Level Principles of Language examination to reach the light of day and so provide an invaluable imprimatur for the classroom testing of the ideas and material to be found in the book. Likewise I am grateful to Peter Downes, the headmaster of Hinchingbrooke School, Huntingdon, and to Duncan Gray of its English Department for involving themselves in the Principles of Language experiment. I also owe thanks to Sarah Lay for help on Japanese.

Professor Eric Hawkins, formerly of the University of York, Professor John Sinclair of the University of Birmingham, David Little of Trinity College, Dublin and Ms Gillian Donmall of King's College, London have been generous with their interest and encouragement over many years. Rosemary Davidson and Keith Rose of the Cambridge University Press have been both tolerant of my erratic regard for deadlines and at the same time constantly encouraging of my efforts.

I hope all the above will accept this traditional mention as a sign of heartfelt gratitude for so much assistance received and all too often inadequately acknowledged, but the final word of thanks must go to Keith, Karen and Stewart Tipping for providing me with family refuge and support during all the days it has taken for this project to come to fruition.

A.J. Tinkel, Reading, October 1987

1 *To the Reader*

The purpose of this book is to make you more alert to language, more cautious about this means of communication that only humans possess. How do they acquire it? How does it function? How do people use it?

However it is impossible to discuss language without considering what happens in particular languages. You cannot examine the human faculty of language without examining how it works in Spanish or Urdu or Welsh. In the case of this book we look at how English works and how English speakers use it.

To be more precise we begin in Chapter **2** by considering what distinguishes language from other ways in which humans communicate. Chapter **3** continues this theme of defining what language is, by examining forms of animal communication and by considering how far some animals can acquire human language. Chapter **4** is an introduction to the way that a baby does acquire it. Chapter **5** considers writing systems and other, similar, means by which we can convey what we want to 'say'. Chapters **6** and **7** look at the natural means of doing so – the spoken word. At the same time in those two chapters we begin to examine how one language in particular functions, namely English. The introduction to the speech sounds of English (Chapter **6**) and to the way English uses pitch and stress (Chapter **7**) is followed by an examination of English grammar. This examination begins (Chapter **8**) with the smallest units of grammar in English that go to make up its nouns (Chapter **9**), its verbs (Chapter **10**), its adjectives (Chapter **11**) and its adverbs (Chapter **12**). The next two chapters consider how those words are put together in simple sentences (Chapter **13**) and in more complicated ones (Chapter **14**). Then Chapter **15** looks at the way English links those sentences together into longer passages. Chapter **16** examines lexical meaning, the kind of meaning on which a traditional dictionary is based. The following chapter, Chapter **17**, moves on to other ways in which we convey meaning, leading into variations in usage (Chapter **18**) and change in language (Chapter **19**). Thus there is an ordered sequence to the chapters, but you do not have to follow it. You will not be at a disadvantage if you wish to skip and select, following your own preferences. The List of Contents is included to help you do this.

You bring to this book your own knowledge of English. Even if you are not able to explain how your language functions, you still use it to communicate and therefore you must know intuitively how it works. The book tries to exploit this fact. It seeks to guide you in exploring that knowledge for yourself. The exploration route is mapped out for you, of course; the sequence of chapter topics has been worked out beforehand, but the material of each chapter is presented to you in the spirit of exploration rather than of repetitive exercise, to encourage you to contribute from your own knowledge and to discover on your own initiative more about the language. Hence the chapter sub-divisions are called Explorations.

Each Exploration is designed to take you through three stages. Firstly there is an explanation of the topic in question; it is made as brief as possible and is supported by examples whenever feasible. You are then given tasks that involve you in the exploration of your own competence in this area. As a result it is hoped you will explore further on your own, using your own experience and your own judgement as a speaker of English.

Some general suggestions for this third stage of further exploration have been included in the book, but since it is the purpose of the final stage to centre your attention on your own language and to hand over to you the initiative in exploring it, they cannot be anything more than broad indications. One suggestion that is mentioned frequently in the text is the keeping of a language *Data Book*. If you are entering fully into the spirit of this third stage, you should keep such a cuttings book of examples of language use that you come across in conversation, on the television or radio, in print or elsewhere and which strike you as interesting.

Guiding you towards exploring your own language experience in your own contexts will go some way to overcoming two constant difficulties that face anyone discussing language on paper. Language is a system that we can use in creative and original ways to an unrestricted extent. As a result it is a system that is constantly changing. Asking you to bring your judgement to bear helps to counter this difficulty. Likewise there is a paradox in trying to discuss the spoken language by means of the written word. Speech conveys meaning in ways that the printed word cannot, but leading you to provide the context of sound yourself helps to resolve the contradiction.

Although the coverage of topics is meant to be comprehensive, it is not meant to be exhaustive. The book is planned as a framework for you to discover more about your own language. But why bother at all? What is the point of finding out more? Are you not in danger of losing more than you gain, when you start thinking about how your language works? Language is so crucial in our lives, however, that it is a natural object of study in its own right. In addition a clearer understanding of what language is and how it functions will help you to counter the many myths and misconceptions that are commonly held about it. Further, by becoming more aware of English sounds, grammar and usage, you will become more sensitive to how you handle the language and how others do as well, and as you explore your understanding of your language you cannot fail to expand it at the same time.

Your language is the key to so much of what you do that a greater awareness of its nature can only be to your advantage.

2 Communication without Language

We start by asking ourselves what constitutes an act of communication. Is communication the same as language? Do we only communicate intentionally? Do we always communicate what we want to? This chapter looks especially at non-language means of communication and how we can analyse them. This chapter is an introduction to the study of signs.

Unconnected with Language

The choices we make about how we wish to live our lives are signalled to others by the outward signs of those choices. What we wear, where we go, what we buy, how we sit, how we stand – these all 'say' something about us, but they say it without any use of language.

Exploration 1 • *Personal Choice*

The kind of clothes you wear; the place you choose for an evening out; the make of car you choose or long for – all these say something about the person behind the choice. These are choices of individual expression, to a greater or lesser degree for conscious effect.

Task | Look at the five pictures in *Figure 1*. What do the various garments tell you about the people wearing them?

Further Exploration

Imagine that you have just won a sum of money on the football pools or in a lottery and that, for the first time in your life, you can afford to buy anything you wish. What image of yourself would you be trying to convey in those circumstances? Collect photographs, advertisements, brochures, etc. for your *Data Book* that illustrate this image.

Figure 1

Exploration 2 • *Social Convention*

These choices can also be made in line with a conventional code, in order to conform with a community expectation. If we go to a funeral we will wear black or dark clothes out of respect for the dead and because the bereaved would be upset if we did not. It is expected that we dress smartly to attend someone's wedding, where we will expect at least the bride to begin wearing a wedding ring. If we turn up for an interview in patched jeans and a paint-stained shirt, our clothes will be taken as an expression of indifference to the interview's outcome, even if this is not what we intend.

Whether the outward signs of these choices are assumed deliberately or unconsciously, whether they show individual expression or social conformity, they communicate information about us, and about our social and cultural attitudes.

Task | Look at the five pictures in *Figure 2*. What role in British society is played by the people who wear these items.

Further Exploration
Collect pictures of other clothing and accessories that have social significance in British society for your *Data Book*. Can you find any examples that are significant in other societies?

Exploration 3 • *Body Language*

The way we hold our body communicates information about ourselves. Drooping shoulders convey depression, a straight back conveys smartness and pride. A person will sit differently on a chair depending on whether they feel at ease, exhausted or obliged to be on their best behaviour. Such postures reflect natural states of our minds and bodies, their needs and desires. We signal our feelings for others through the way in which we hold our body and look for such signals ourselves as evidence of the feelings of others towards us. If we lean forward to listen, our body is signalling our interest in what is being said. If we are slumped back or leaning back on our chair, we are conveying the opposite.

Task | Look at the five pictures in *Figure 3*. What state of mind do you think is being conveyed by the body posture of the people in the photographs?

Figure 2

Figure 3

Further exploration

Collect illustrations of expressive body postures for your *Data Book*.

Collect advertisements containing pictures of men or women. What do their body postures aim to convey to you? What image does the advertiser aim to persuade you that you will acquire if you purchase the item? What elements in the advertisement lead you to that conclusion?

Associated with Language

Exploration 4 • *Voice and Body*

When we talk we put language into sound, but our voice also gives the listener information about our physical condition. Whether on the telephone, on tape or on the radio, the listener can usually tell whether it is a man, a woman or a child who is talking, what their age group is, and whether they have any distinguishing features in their speech. The listener will also make a judgement about the quality of the voice – whether it is gruff or smooth, deep or high-pitched.

Task | Make a tape recording of five people of different ages and sex. Ask your group to guess the age and sex of each speaker. Can you deduce any further information about the speakers from the recordings?

Task | Make tape recordings of your family and friends at home, and take them into your language group for the others to identify. Which kinds of voice are easiest to identify, and which the most difficult?

Exploration 5 • *Voice and Mind*

Our voice also reflects our state of mind when we speak. The listener can tell whether we are indifferent, distraught, tense or pleased. We can use exactly the same words when we are bored or when we are angry, and our boredom or anger will communicate itself through our voice. It is possible for us to add this kind of emotional colouring to our voice consciously. We can act as if we are angry. It is also possible for us to suppress it. We can pretend we are not bored. However for the most part we convey such information without realising that we are doing so.

Task | Make a tape recording of five different people displaying different moods. Ask your group to estimate the emotional state of each speaker.

Further Exploration

Identify and record further examples of voices conveying different physical and emotional states. Prepare them for your fellow students to analyse.

Exploration 6 • *Vocal Gestures*

We can use our speech mechanism of tongue, teeth, etc. to make meaningful noises that are independent of a language. A whistle of surprise, a tut-tut click of disapproval with the tip of the tongue, and a sucking-in of air through the teeth in apprehension are all sounds made by English speakers with parts of the speech mechanism, but they are not speech sounds of English in the same way that /p/, /b/ and /d/ are. In English we can say *sh* to someone to tell them to be quiet, but the same noise is also the first speech sound in *shop*, *sheep* and *shut*.

Task | Make a tape recording of five different vocal gestures. Ask your group to guess what information is being conveyed in each case. What part of the speech mechanism is producing the sound?

Further Exploration

List 'words' in English that attempt to capture on paper sounds that we can make with our speech mechanism – whether deliberately or not – but which are not regarded as words of the English language, e.g. *ouch* for a cry of pain. Are these 'words' included in a dictionary?

Exploration 7 • *Non-vocal Sound Gestures*

Sounds that convey meaning independently of a language are not restricted to examples produced by the speech mechanism. A click of the fingers to attract attention, clapping of the hands in applause, tapping the feet with impatience, and a knock at the door all give information.

Task | List ten different noises made by the hands or the feet which convey information.

Further Exploration

Make a list of sound gestures, both vocal and non-vocal, that are directed at the sense of hearing for your *Data Book*. Consider whether they are culture-specific. Would they be understood by anybody or are they restricted to English speakers? In the latter case would all English speakers understand them? If so, would they understand them in the same way?

Which of the gestures you have listed would normally be made deliberately and which ones are likely to be involuntary? How far would this depend on the context in which the gestures were made?

Exploration 8 • *Facial Expressions*

Facial expressions can be used to communicate a meaning. We can wink knowingly, screw up our nose in disgust, frown in incomprehension, or poke out our tongue in contempt.

Task | Look at the five pictures in *Figure 4*. What meaning does each one convey?

Further Exploration

Collect newspaper photographs of faces which illustrate the following: anger, indifference, sadness, joy, tiredness, boredom, friendliness, worry, arrogance, tension, dejection, determination, slyness, curiosity, fear, viciousness, gentleness, contentment, wonder, threat. Can you fit each of the photographs into just one of these categories or do you need more information about the context?

List those facial expressions that you would consider to be deliberate gestures, e.g. a knowing wink, as opposed to reflections of a person's state of mind, e.g. a tired expression. To what extent will your decision depend on the context in which each expression is made?

Exploration 9 • *Gestures with Limbs and Head*

Gestures of the hand or other parts of the body can communicate a meaning, as when we beckon to someone with our hand, or shake our head.

Task | Look at the five hand gestures in *Figure 5*. Can you give a meaning to each one? How much variation in meaning is possible?

Figure 4

Figure 5

Further Exploration

List gestures that could be used among English speakers to convey the following: 'stop', 'I don't know', 'slow down', 'we're going to win', 'you are an idiot', 'come here', 'that one there', 'I give up', 'I don't want to hear', 'it is very cold'.

Think of as many different gestures of greeting as possible. What restrictions are there on their meaning and/or use? How far are they culture-specific?

Make a list of gestures that are made by parts of the body other than the hands, e.g. a shrug of the shoulders or a nod of the head.

Exploration 10 • *Gestures by Touch*

All of the gestures we have mentioned so far have been vocal or visual, but gestures can also be directed at the sense of touch, as when we pat someone on the shoulder in congratulation, tap someone's ankle under the table in warning, or nudge someone with our elbow in search of support and agreement.

Task | Which of the following verbs can indicate gesturing by touch?
frown, stroke, pinch, wave, scowl, jostle, pat, kiss, slap, laugh.

Further Exploration

Make a list of gestures that rely on the receiver's sense of touch.

Exploration 11 • *Combining Gestures*

Gestures can be combined with vocal sounds and facial expressions to communicate a meaning, as when we cover our ears and tense our face to keep out a piercing sound; thumb our nose, poke out our tongue and make a mocking noise; say *ugh* and pinch our nose in defence against a bad smell. Likewise gestures and expressions accompany speech.

Task | Imagine yourself in a position where you are unable to speak, but you can make sounds through your speech mechanism to convey your meaning. How will you convey the following concepts in such circumstances? 'No', 'I question that', 'yes', 'emphatic no', 'I don't like that', 'emphatic yes', 'I am fed up with this', 'hesitation', 'I like that', 'that hurts'. How far will you rely on other gestures accompanying the sounds to make your meaning clear?

Further Exploration

Make a list of signs that convey meaning among English speakers by combining a gesture of the hand(s) with a facial expression and/or a vocal sound.

Exploration 12 • *Pictorial and Arbitrary*

A gesture can have a pictorial connection with its meaning, as in beckoning someone to approach or clenching the fist in threat. Many gestures, however, have no such pictorial connection for us when we use them. Although there may originally have been a pictorial connection between a nod of the head and the idea of acceptance, between joined hands and prayer, between thumbs pointing downwards and bad news, for today's user of such gestures the connection is much more likely to be an arbitrary one, established by convention and use.

Task | Look at *Figure 6*. It contains ten gestures from the sign system of the North American Indians, as quoted by Theodore Brun in *The International Dictionary of Sign Language*. Work out which gesture conveys each of the following messages:

a. 'I'
b. 'cry/grieve'
c. 'peace'
d. 'future/after'
e. 'no'
f. 'shrink back/fear'
g. 'bad/throw away'
h. 'sun'
i. 'add'
j. 'question'

Further Exploration

Make a list of gestures or facial expressions that would be understandable to those unfamiliar with them, because they contain a clear pictorial link with the meaning they convey. Are these gestures likely to be culture-specific?

Figure 6

Exploration 13 • *Voluntary and Involuntary Gestures*

Some facial expressions, sounds and movements are made unconsciously, even involuntarily. Our leg makes a reflex movement when a certain part of the lower knee is struck; we start at a loud noise or when a sensitive spot is touched; our eyelids will droop if we are very tired. Such physical reactions we can do little to prevent. We can do more to control gestures and expressions, such as a furrowed brow if we are worried, or fidgety fingers if we are impatient, or a look of disinterest if we are bored, which we nevertheless normally produce without being fully aware of doing so. In addition we each have our own expressions and gestures peculiar to ourselves, which, like the quality of our voice, are part of the individual picture we present to the world, but which we produce as unconscious habits.

Task | Which of the following verbs indicate an involuntary physical reaction and which convey a conscious gesture?

jump, yawn, sneeze, sniff, sigh, whistle, groan, nod, belch, hiss.

Which of these verbs can be used in either sense, depending on the context?

Consider what the following can convey to the observer/hearer in the English-speaking world, bearing in mind that there may be more than one interpretation in each case. If necessary, define the context more closely before answering. State whether the communication involved is being conveyed as a deliberate act, or is more likely to be an unconscious act.

a. closed eyelids
b. right index finger placed over closed lips
c. the tips of the fingers and thumb of the right hand brought together, moved to the mouth, kissed and then opened out as the hand is taken away
d. thumb and index finger squeezing nostrils
e. right and left thumbs placed against right and left temples, palms facing the onlooker, and fingers moving up and down
f. a sucking-in of air through clenched teeth

Further Exploration

Analyse your own habitual gestures and those of your group.

Analyse the gestures traditionally used in a different culture, e.g. by Italians, Chinese or Arabs. Are there any differences? Are there any similarities? Do the differences and similarities help you to decide whether these gestures are pictorial or arbitrary?

Exploration 14 • *Paralanguage*

This whole area of communication that exists side by side with speech and very often supplements it, is called paralanguage.

Imagine that you are in a situation where visual communication is going to be more effective than the spoken word. Such a context could be a crowded room at a party, or on the tarmac of an airport near aircraft engines, or through the plate glass window of a recording studio. How would you convey the following messages with gestures?

a. 'Stop'
b. 'Come forward very slowly'
c. 'Don't look round'
d. 'Move five metres to your left'
e. 'What is the matter with your right hand?'
f. 'How many helpers do you require?'
g. 'Bring your companion over here in ten minutes' time'
h. 'What is his name?'
i. 'You have the wrong jacket on'
j. 'Your salary cheque is in the office'

State in each case whether you think the gestures you use are arbitrary or have a pictorial link with the meaning. Comment on the difficulty of finding an appropriate gesture or set of gestures for each of the meanings. Which meanings would be conveyed better through (spoken) language? How much are you relying on the context?

Further Exploration

Analyse methods of communication used in advertising that do not use language.

Signs

Exploration 15 • *Signs and Significance*

As soon as a colour or an object or a movement – in short any phenomenon that the senses recognise – begins to refer to something beyond its own existence, it becomes a sign or a symbol. Roses, thistles, daffodils and shamrock are plants, but they are also signs for England, Scotland, Wales and Ireland. An eagle can be used to represent the United States of America and a kiwi New Zealand. Red is a primary colour, but it is also a sign for danger or for coming to a halt. A thumb is part of the body that becomes a sign of approval if turned upwards or disapproval if turned down.

Task | State the countries that are frequently identified by the following: bear, maple leaf, cock, red dragon, chrysanthemums, springbok, pyramids, white cross on red, kangaroo, the colour orange.

Task | Which human characteristics are associated with the following colours: black, green, red, blue, yellow?

Task | The following parts of the human body are traditionally the seat of which human emotions or qualities: heart, liver, spleen, stomach, head?

Task | Give examples of how English usage reflects these links between human characteristics and colours and between emotions or qualities and parts of the body, as for example in 'Can you give me a hand, please?'

Further Explorations

Collect examples in other areas where physical phenomena commonly have a value as signs or symbols.

Exploration 16 • *Indexical Signs*

Signs can have a natural and inevitable link with the thing they signify. Dark clouds mean that rain is coming; a swollen river means that a lot of rain has fallen; footprints outside a door mean that someone has been there; a queue of cars indicates a blockage ahead. The sign in such cases is an automatic product of what it signifies and it has not been invested with any extra significance. Such an inescapable link means that no surprise information is communicated by the appearance of such signs. They are on a par with involuntary kinds of human communication referred to in 2 Exploration 13, such as a yawn indicating tiredness and a cry of *ouch* indicating pain. They point in one constant direction for an explanation of their meaning and are sometimes called an 'index' as a result.

Task | Sherlock Holmes' powers of deduction relied heavily on his interpretation of indexical signs. Collect some examples from the stories for your *Data Book*.

Further Exploration

To what extent could the indexical signs that you have identified be manipulated in order to mislead, as, for example, the fugitive horseman who shod his horse back to front to send his pursuers in the wrong direction?

Exploration 17 • *Pictorial Signs*

We saw in 2 Exploration 12 that some of the sounds, gestures and facial expressions that we use consciously for communication carry a pictorial link with the thing they signify, such as the pop-pop-pop sound made by the lips to indicate liquid pouring from a bottle and hence a drink, or drawing the side of the hand across the throat to indicate extreme displeasure, or lowering the eyelids to indicate unwillingness to see something.

Many signs contain a pictorial connection with the thing they represent. In *Figure 7* the road traffic signs to warn of 'crossroads', 'slippery road', 'traffic lights' and 'pedestrian crossing' are comprehensible at once even if unfamiliar, because there is a clear pictorial link with the meaning. Such signs are sometimes termed 'iconic'.

Task | In *Figure 8* there are five flags. Can you identify them? Are you aware of the reasons that lie behind the choice of shapes and colours? If you were not aware of them, could you have deduced their significance?

Figure 7

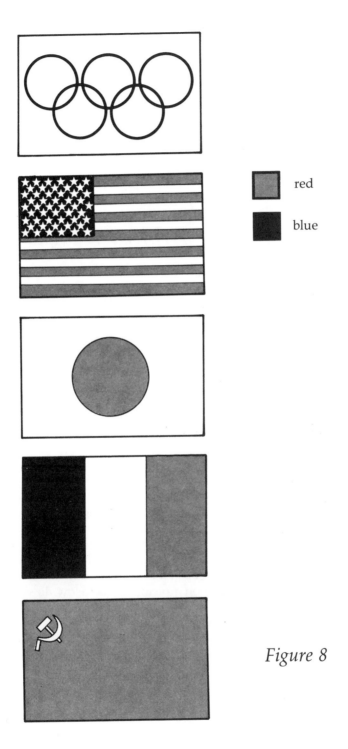

red

blue

Figure 8

Further Exploration

Collect logos of organisations, companies, etc. How far is an organisation's logo connected pictorially with its sphere of activity? How far is the logo dependent for its significance on being placed next to an identifying word? How far is a special typeface used for identification? How far is colour used for identification? How far can colour and typeface be considered as signs in themselves? If a logo has no pictorial association for you, but you nevertheless recognised it, find out how long it has been used and in what context you first came across it. Did it originally have any pictorial association with the company's activities? Can words or initials be considered as signs in themselves, regardless of shape or colour?

Exploration 18 • *Arbitrary Signs*

The other four road traffic signs in *Figure 7* – 'no entry', 'no stopping', 'give way', 'warning (exclamation mark)' – contain no pictorial element to link them with the thing they signify. That link is an arbitrary one, established by convention. The meaning of such signs must either be known in advance, as in 'no entry' and 'end of speed restriction', or they must be explained with words that will be understood. The use of any arbitrary sign, whether external, facial expression, gesture or sound, is restricted by the need to communicate. A sign will not mean anything unless other people, apart from the originator, know what it means. There must be, as it were, an agreement (or convention) about what such a sign means, before it can be used. Hence such signs, when established, are not only arbitrary, but also conventional.

Task | Imagine that you have been asked by the organising committee of an international conference to design signs for the various conference facilities listed below. Make a sketch drawing of each sign, bearing in mind that not all of those attending the conference will be able to understand English and that they will belong to the widest possible variety of cultures. Consider in each case whether your sign has a pictorial link with its meaning, and whether there are any cultural restrictions on the use of that link. What difficulties do you encounter when you cannot rely on a pictorial link? How do you handle a facility that contains more than one concept in its designation? The facilities are 'car park', 'conference office', 'toilets', 'TV rooms', 'postal facilities', 'courtesy bus to the local town', 'showers', 'self-service cafeteria', 'reading room', 'silent meditation room'.

Task | You have been asked to design a set of signs to represent different types of weather in a television weather forecast. In designing signs to represent the following types of weather, state which ones can be directly represented pictorially, which ones can be best represented by a picture of something associated with that weather, and which ones defy any kind of pictorial depiction and require a word or other arbitrary sign to convey their meaning. The weather types are 'rain', 'wind', 'fog', 'snow', 'low temperature', 'high temperature', 'sun', 'cloudy', 'showers and bright intervals', 'thunder and lightning'.

Further Exploration

Look at heraldic coats of arms. Identify in them examples of signs that refer to the life, work or other circumstances of the person originally granted the coat of arms. If the coats of arms were granted to a town, district or institution, are there any symbolic references to it contained in the design, as for example an ox above water in the arms of the city of Oxford?

Identify also examples of a rebus – a picture of an object whose name recalls the name of the person or institution – as for example stylised snowflakes in the coat of arms of Lord Snow, or the traditional children's joke of conveying 'Tony' by pointing to the toe and then the knee.

Exploration 19 • *Gestures as Signs*

We saw in 2 Exploration 18 that gesture, facial expression and non-speech sound are signs, if we use them to communicate. Communication is a two-way process. We send information out, but we also receive it. Our gestures are other people's external signs, just as much as the road traffic signs and national symbols referred to above. However these are a restricted form of communication, since they do not have the possibility of being extended and varied in their meaning and use, and they cannot be combined to make a different sign.

Task | Identify ten instances where a gesture, sound or facial expression has been adopted for wider use as a sign, as for example the adoption by the Abbey National Building Society of a stylised thumbs-up of approval or the use of a pointing hand rather than an arrow to indicate direction.

---

3 Animal Communication

We can now go on to look at aspects of communication in other species. Is it valid to say that animals communicate with each other? Do they use the same means of communication as humans? Do they have language? We look at some interesting attempts to teach animals a human-like language.

Exploration 1 • *All Living Beings Communicate*

The ability to communicate is not the exclusive possession of human beings. Even at the level of existence of the amoeba communication takes place. A chemical discharge from one amoeba attracts others to it for the cellular aggregation necessary for reproduction.

In their courtship ritual, spiders use vibrations of the web to communicate, together with visual displays at close quarters and the release of chemical stimuli. The male spider can detect by scent the sex and species of the spider inside a web, but it also needs to know whether a female will accept its advances. It is important that the male learn quickly and clearly about the sexual readiness of the female in the web, otherwise he will be attacked.

Fireflies exchange light flashes for their courtship rituals. The male flies in the air and signals. If the female on the ground replies after the correct interval, the male continues the exchange and begins to approach.

Fish communicate by visual means when enough light penetrates the water, but when the water is muddy or the fish are at greater depths other means must be used. A frightened minnow will let out a substance that stimulates a frightened reaction in other fish of the species. Some tropical fish use electric pulses for orientation and it is possible that such signals have a communicative function as well. Fish react to differences in pressure waves through the water, which they monitor through the swim bladder.

Birds use sounds – their song – to communicate in courtship, between parent and young, and between others of the same species. Birdsong is used to announce the presence of a male; it helps the male to find a mate of the right species and to deter other males from invading his territory. Call notes are used for passing on information. They warn of danger, help control the movement of the flock, and indicate the whereabouts of food. Birdsong serves both as an individual and as a species signal.

The humpbacked whale produces a song during migration that lasts about ten minutes and which identifies its presence to other humpbacked whales within hearing distance. As the sound they make is carried long distances under water, that hearing distance covers a wide area.

Task | All these examples of animal communication revolve around the immediate needs of the animal – the desire to mate, the desire to protect itself and survive, and the desire to obtain food. Identify the different ways in which the information is conveyed or sought in these examples.

Further Reading

Animal Nature and Human Nature, W. H. Thorpe, Methuen, 1974.

Exploration 2 • *Animals and Creativity*

It is not the sophisticated nature or otherwise of a means of animal communication that is particularly interesting to the student of human language, but whether it is possible for an animal to communicate a message which does not depend upon the stimulus of the immediate context; a message not necessarily related to the immediate context and one that is beyond the fixed set of responses expected of its species. Can an animal convey and receive information unrelated to its immediate needs? Can it choose what it communicates? Can an animal be individually creative in what it communicates?

Task | Consider the following examples of animals communicating. Can any of them be described as arbitrary or conventional?

– a cat rubbing against a person in affection, a robin's song to warn other robins to keep away from its territory, a peacock displaying its tail to attract a mate, a dog baring its teeth in threat, a porcupine raising and rattling its quills, a cat purring in contentment, a dog barking a warning, a bull lowering its head and charging, a cow mooing because it hasn't been milked, a fox marking out its territory with scent from its brush.

Further Exploration

Listen to recordings of birdsongs on tape. Compare the recordings of the mating songs of birds with those of the territorial defence songs of the same birds. What difference can you detect between the two songs of each bird?

Select an investigation into the communication system of an animal species and examine it to find out how far that species' communication extends beyond the urge to mate and the need to survive.

Exploration 3 • *Training Animals*

When a dog has learnt to respond to the command *sit*, or to bring the morning newspaper in its mouth, it has responded to training. So too has the horse, when it reacts as desired to sensitive movements of the reins, and the cat, when it learns to use the cat litter and returns to the house for its food at the same time every day. We are teaching animals behaviour outside their normal limits, when we adapt them to our service and lifestyle. Music hall turns or circus tricks with animals are a more spectacular version of their training potential.

Such training produces behaviour in an animal which is unprompted by a natural stimulus in a specific content, and can even lead to creative behaviour, e.g. when a dog fetches help for its injured and unconscious keeper. However the communication involved in such behaviour still cannot be termed human language in any strict sense. We feel we have to look beyond the conditioned responses that underlie such training, even when it leads to intelligent behaviour, to test whether animals are capable of language. Lack of physical stimulus and an element of creativity are not a precise enough characterisation of language.

Task | When a shepherd teaches a sheepdog to respond to certain whistles and commands, can the shepherd be said to be teaching it a language?

Exploration 4 • *Training Children*

The father of a young baby just learning to talk once taught his child to pronounce the word *marsupial*. He then taught the baby to say the word in answer to *What kind of mammal is a kangaroo?*, as mock proof of its precocious intelligence. The baby was taught the word as a joke and the humour lay in the fact that 'marsupial' as a concept is one that only an older child can be expected to express.

Task | Eleven-year-old pupils are likely to encounter the following terms in the classroom in the course of their lessons:

soil erosion, direct object, algebraic equation, chemical solution, renaissance, adjectival agreement, negative pole, theory of evolution, abridged version, economic development.

Which of these terms would you expect a pupil to recognise on first hearing? Which of the concepts underlying these terms would you expect a pupil of this age to understand fully? If the concepts were not understood, how would you explain them, so that the pupil could grasp them? What other terms can you think of, that an 11-year-old pupil is likely to encounter which would need explanation? Do you think that these pupils can use terms that they do not understand in an appropriate way? Can they use such terms creatively in new sentences and contexts?

Exploration 5 • *Animals and Human Language*

During the last 50 years or so a number of experiments have been conducted to see whether an animal is capable of acquiring some form of human language. The subjects of these experiments have been either chimpanzees or, in one case, a gorilla, since it was felt that primates, as our closest relations in the animal kingdom, offered the greatest chance of success.

Winthrop and Luella Kellogg brought up their baby son in the company of an infant chimpanzee called Gua. At sixteen months Gua could understand about a hundred spoken words, more than the Kelloggs' son at that age, but she did not progress further.

The Kelloggs' experiment only involved the chimpanzee in understanding. After the Second World War Keith and Catherine Hayes tried to teach a chimpanzee to talk as well as understand, but after six years of the experiment she could only manage to produce three or four words that could be recognised.

Allen and Beatrice Gardner tried a different approach with their infant chimpanzee, Washoe. They 'talked' to it by means of Ameslan (American Sign Language). By the age of four it could produce as well as understand 87 signs and had made 294 two-sign combinations, such as those meaning 'more fruit' and 'please tickle'.

A little later than the Gardners, Ann James Premack and David Premack began an experiment with a chimpanzee called Sarah. This experiment differed from the preceding ones in that Sarah was taught not by means of speech or signing, but by means of plastic pieces that varied in shape and colour and to which particular meanings had been attached in her mind. The experiment set out to explore Sarah's ability to grasp more advanced linguistic concepts, such as 'name-of', 'same-as' and conditional statements, as well as more straightforward ones like 'apple', 'pail' and 'give'. Sarah learned some 130 terms of both levels of difficulty and was able to understand sentences such as: 'If Mary takes red (the symbol for which was coloured grey), then Sarah (can) take (the) apple', or 'Sarah insert (the) apple (in the) pail (and the) banana (in the) dish'.

Duane Rumbaugh taught Lana to push buttons on a computer console. Each button had a symbol on it, and Lana learned to press the buttons in sequences, like 'please machine give Lana piece of apple'.

Francine Patterson's experiment began in 1972, when she started to teach Koko, a young gorilla, by means of Ameslan sign language. This was a continuation of the Gardners' approach, aiming at both the understanding of the signs by the ape and the production of sign utterances in return. This experiment has, however, been more ambitious, and Koko learned several hundred signs. It has lasted longer, brought the animal more closely into the lives of the trainers and involved a greater number of people.

Task | Study the primate experiments listed above. Do they show a level of communication above that of a sheepdog responding to a whistle? Do they show any of the features of human language? Which features of human language do they not show?

Further Reading

Details of these experiments can be found in:

The Ape and the Child, W. N. Kellogg and Luella A. Kellogg, McGraw-Hill, 1933.

The Ape in Our House, Catherine Hayes, Harper, 1951.

'Teaching Sign Language to a Chimpanzee', R. A. Gardner and B. T. Gardner *Science* 165, August 1969.

'Teaching Language to an Ape', Ann James Premack and David Premack, *Scientific American*, October 1972.

Acquisition of Linguistic Skills by a Chimpanzee, D. M. Rumbaugh, Academic Press, 1977.

The Education of Koko, Francine Patterson and Eugene Linden, André Deutsch, 1982.

Apes, Men and Language, Eugene Linden, Penguin, 1981.

Animal Nature and Human Nature, W. H. Thorpe, Methuen, 1974.

4 *First Language Acquisition*

We can now look again at some of the assumptions we have been making about language and language learning, by looking at how children learn language. Do we, in fact, 'teach' children language?

Exploration 1 • *Approximate Stages in the Acquisition Process*

A child acquires its mother tongue in a series of stages that are similar in children all over the world. These stages take place irrespective of the kind of society the child is born into, the level of intelligence it later displays, the language it is learning to speak or the culture it is growing up in. The child will acquire the language which is being spoken by the people who surround it, but it will do so in a way that resembles another child acquiring a different language.

At the same time the process of acquisition in one child will not follow an identical timetable to that of another child. Some children reach a stage of language acquisition at an earlier age than others; other children are late developers, but may then move through stages more rapidly.

Stage 1 At the beginning of its first year of life the child uses sounds to communicate simple needs and wants. It cries, screams and makes general noises of discontent.

Stage 2 Somewhere around the age of three months the child begins to expand its range of sounds. It is embarking on the 'babbling' stage, when it is no longer merely making noises to communicate hunger, pain and annoyance. It begins to make sounds for their own sake; it begins to enjoy exploring the range of sounds its vocal organs can make. It is, as it were, limbering up these organs for the task ahead.

Stage 3 This exploration of sounds develops and expands to include an imitation of intonation patterns. Then, sometime approaching the age of twelve months, the child begins to assemble sounds in sequences and to attach meanings to these sequences. It is beginning to utter its first 'words'. At this stage these sequences are not really like adult words, but they nevertheless represent the emergence of an ability to relate sound to meaning. When the child says *dada*, it may not even be referring to a man, let alone its father, but it is referring to something.

Stage 4 This ability to relate sound to meaning develops during the child's second year of life. Vocabulary expands and reference becomes more precise, until by the child's second birthday it is using words with recognisable adult references. These words are also, by this time, being put together in sentences. First of all the sentences are formed out of two or three words only. These two-word sentences are not imitations of what the child hears adults say; they sound like extracts from a telegram or a newspaper headline: *Ball gone, More jam, Sock dirty*. But even these two-word sentences are governed by rules. The child will not put words together at random, but will select combinations according to these rules. This, added to the fact that the child is not imitating adult speech, suggests that the child is forming its sentences according to some sort of system.

New words, which are being acquired at the same time, are fitted into the pattern of sentence structure being developed, enabling the child to form sentences that it has not used or heard before. If it learnt the words *teddy, bread, clean*, it can produce the sentences *Teddy gone, More bread, Sock clean*. The child has the beginnings of a communication system that it can adapt for itself to create and produce new sentences.

Stage 5 The length of the child's sentences grows during its third year of life, but they are still not identical to adult speech in form. Between the ages of two and four its sentence structure is gradually brought into line with that of an adult. It learns where to insert linking words like *is, to, by*, and where to add inflections like *-ing* in *going* and *-s* in *tables*. It learns to ask questions and to form a negative. In each case the sentences suggest that the child is developing a rule-governed system in its mind.

Stage 6 By its fifth year of life the child controls most of the English sounds of speech. Its vocabulary has expanded rapidly since its second birthday and it commands the basic English sentence patterns. The child will continue to extend its range of vocabulary and sentence pattern, as it grows up and matures, but by the age of five it has acquired the basic sounds, words and structures of the language.

Task Although, after the age of four, the child can control the sounds of English, it may sometimes have difficulty in pronouncing clusters of consonants, such as *str* or *ngths*. List ten words that could contain this difficulty and which are likely to be used by a four-and-a-half-year-old.

Task | When the child learns that *-ed/d* is placed on the end of a verb to indicate past time, it begins by assuming that this rule applies to all verbs. Only later does it learn the irregular exceptions. What past tense forms of the following verbs would you therefore expect a child to produce, when it has only just mastered the use of this ending: *break, teach, go, do, leave, throw, see, catch, put, write*? What does this tell us about the child's language system?

Task | Consider how a baby's language acquisition might be affected if it is born:
a. without hearing
b. without sight
c. without the ability to make speech sounds?

Exploration 2 • *External Factors and Language Acquisition*

In Exploration 1 the emphasis was placed on the child's development of an internal system in its acquisition of language. External social factors are also important for the child's learning of its first language. The child learns the language that it hears spoken around it, and if it is not exposed to a language used by others, it does not acquire language of its own. It must have contact with people who talk. Whatever part the mind of the child plays in its acquisition of language, it can only play that part when it is exposed to people using a language with it and around it.

Task | What conclusions about bringing up children can be drawn from the statements in the previous paragraph?

Further Exploration

Read up and compare the two following cases of child neglect. What differences are there between the two cases in the way the first language acquisition of each child was affected? Why might this be the case?

Isabelle Isabelle was the illegitimate child of a deaf-mute. She was discovered in the 1930s in Ohio, when she was six-and-a-half. She had no speech and made only a croaking sound. She had spent most of her time with her mother in a darkened room, but once she was brought out into contact with users of language, she rapidly learned to talk and by eight-and-a-half had caught up with children of her own age.

Genie Genie was isolated from human language while she was growing up. Her father kept her confined and without language contact, so that when she was discovered – after the onset of adolescence – she was unable to speak. Genie had great difficulty in learning to speak after she came into contact with language.

Further Reading

Language in Infancy and Childhood, Alan Cruttenden, Manchester University Press, 1979.

The Articulate Mammal, Jean Aitchison, Hutchinson, 1976.

Early Language, Peter A. de Villiers and Jill G. de Villiers, Fontana/Open Books, 1979.

A tape with examples of child language acquisition accompanies *Introduction to Language*, T. R. W. Aplin, J. W. Crawshaw, E. A. Roselman and A. L. Williams, Hodder and Stoughton, 1981.

Details of the case of Isabelle can be found in *Words and Things*, R. Brown, The Free Press, 1958; and of Genie in *The Linguistic Development of Genie*, S Curtiss, V. Fromkin, S. Krashen, D. Rigler and M. Rigler, *Language* 50 (1974), pages 528–54.

5 *Language: Form and Substance*

We have already seen that language is only one means of communication. Similarly, speech is only one way of conveying language. Is it possible for people who can't speak to have access to the same language as people who can? We look here at the development of writing systems, including alphabets for special groups and for special purposes.

Exploration 1 • *Speech and Language*

Although speech is the natural means of expressing a language, it is not synonymous with language. Speech sound is the most complete means we possess of expressing language, but it must be seen as something distinct from language. The terminology normally used to express the distinction between language and the vehicle that carries it, is that language is 'form' and the vehicle – whether it be speech sound or anything else – is 'substance'. The word 'form' is intended to convey that language is an abstract system. We can only use this abstract system when it is carried by a physically measurable substance, but it can be brought into the physical world by different substances.

Task | What devices have been developed for people to communicate by means of language when they are:

1. blind
2. deaf
3. unable to articulate speech sounds?

In what circumstances are these devices a necessary substitute for speech? In what circumstances are they superfluous, in that the people handicapped in the three ways mentioned do not need them for communication either through language or more generally?

What devices have been developed to convey language when speech is temporarily out of the question? State how speech can be replaced when sight, sight and hearing (but not the hearing of speech), or sight over a considerable distance are the only senses that can be used?

What devices have been developed to overcome the fact that speech fades rapidly? What kind of reasons have created the need for them, do you think?

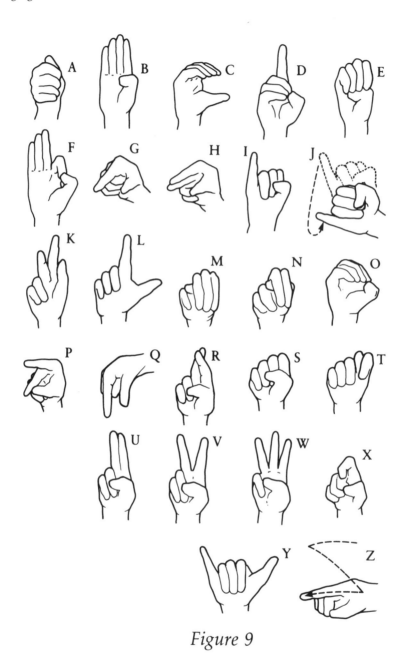

Figure 9

In *Figure 9* you see the American Manual Sign Alphabet. Using this alphabet, make for yourself the 'words' for 'drink', 'eat', 'bean', 'cat', 'please', 'baby', 'time', 'love', 'necklace' and 'man'.

What signs would you expect the American Manual Sign Alphabet to have developed, in the interests of greater speed of communication, for 'eye', 'under', 'fish', 'reject', 'trousers', 'bite', 'ring', 'write', 'quiet', 'cut'? Are any of the signs you have conjectured of an arbitrary nature?

Further Exploration

Those wishing to know more about various sign languages for the deaf and hard of hearing should contact the Royal National Institute for the Deaf, 105 Gower Street, London WC1E 6AH.

Further Reading

American Sign Language and Sign Systems, Ronnie Bring Wilbur, University Park Press, Baltimore, 1979.

Exploration 2 • *Writing and Signs*

Even when there is no problem of physical disability, speech may not necessarily be the most suitable substance. It lacks permanence, cannot carry over a long distance and can be submerged by other noises. Writing developed to overcome these disadvantages and thereby to constitute an alternative substance for language.

We saw in 2 Exploration 17 (*Figure 7*) examples of road traffic signs like 'pedestrian crossing' or 'traffic lights' which presented a straightforward picture of the object to the motorist. Other road traffic signs, like 'crossroads' or 'slippery road', presented a more stylised picture, while the signs for 'no entry' and 'warning' had a conventional and arbitrary link with the meaning without any pictorial representation. What they have in common, however, is that they represent ideas, not language. The sign in *Figure 7* for 'ford' or the specification of 'fallen tree' as the danger under the warning sign also constitute conventional and arbitrary representations, but ones that refer to the English language conveying them. We have moved from signs to language substance when that is the case.

Exploration 3 • *The Development of Writing*

Writing developed many years, possibly thousands of years, after speech. Even today there are many millions of people who have a spoken language with no written form. Writing developed from pictures of objects. These pictures became signs which were used to stand for the objects themselves. Inevitably such signs became more stylised with widening use. As a result they gradually became less connected visually with the objects they represented. The Chinese writing system contains signs which are stylised drawings of objects. In Chinese script 'moon' has developed from 〇 to 月 , 'mountain' from 〇 to 山 .

   Such pictographic signs had to be supplemented by ideographic signs, representing mental concepts as opposed to physical objects, if a system of signs was to be an adequate vehicle for expressing human thinking. The road traffic sign for 'slippery road' (*Figure 7*) is conveying an idea of slipperiness through a picture of the result of the slipperiness. It is not a picture of slipperiness itself, but of a typical outcome on the roads.

Task | Look at the keyboard of any typewriter. In addition to letters of the alphabet, there are a number of signs on it. List ten of them with their meanings. State whether you consider them to be ideograms representing a concept, as £ represents 'pound sterling', or logograms representing a word, as @ represents 'at'. To what extent can the signs that you have chosen be seen as examples of both?

Further Exploration

The earliest known writing system was developed by the Sumerians in Mesopotamia about five thousand years ago. It began as a set of pictograms, e.g. 〈〈 for 'fish' and 〇 for 'corn', but became a system of stylised signs that could be impressed easily on wet clay tablets with a reed. The tablets would then be dried in the sun. This script is called *cuneiform*. When Akkadian replaced Sumerian as a spoken language in the area, the Sumerian cuneiform system of writing was adapted to Akkadian.

   The Egyptians were evolving their own system of writing at about the same time as the Sumerians and it began with the pictograms we know as *hieroglyphics*. They were recorded on material made from the stem of the papyrus (paper reed) by means of a slender rush.

Task | Investigate the early history of writing with particular reference to
     | cuneiform and hieroglyphics.

Task | What are the limitations of a pictographic or hieroglyphic writing
     | system? How many symbols would you need to carry out your daily
     | tasks if we still used such a writing system today?

Further Reading

Hieroglyphs to Alphabets, Charles King, Fred. Muller

Problems in the Origins and Development of the English Language, John Algeo,
Harcourt Brace Jovanovich, 1972.

Exploration 4 • *Speech Sound and Script*

The rebus principle described in 2 Exploration 18 can be used to portray the
spoken word. For example a picture of a slipper and a ness, or headland, could
be used to portray the spoken form 'slipperiness'. A picture of the sun could
represent not only the spoken form of the word 'sun', but also the
similar-sounding spoken form of 'son'. The important principle here is that the
written form no longer bears any pictorial relationship to the spoken form. It
has become arbitrary. The rebus device uses an awareness of the sounds of a
language, rather than a direct reference to the meaning involved.

As soon as a system of pictographic or ideographic signs included elements
of any kind that referred to the sounds of spoken language (phonetic signs),
the signs ceased to be simply representations of meanings and began to mirror
the workings of a language. They became a vehicle for language, not a
succession of communication signs.

Exploration 5 • *Syllabic Writing*

The inclusion in writing systems of a phonetic element – a reference to the
sound made in speaking – opened up possibilities for simplification and greater
precision. Signs referring to the pronunciation of words rather than the ideas
behind them were developed for this reason in both the Egyptian and the
Sumerian-Akkadian writing systems. These developments were in the form of
signs to represent syllables, and they existed alongside the earlier logographic
signs.

Task | Imagine that English was written with a syllabic system and not an
alphabetic one. Taking capital letters to represent syllables in the words
below, rewrite the words according to this syllabary. For example, if
A = *car*, B = *park*, C = *key*, D = *side*, then in this syllabary AB = *carpark*,
BD = *parkside*, CD = *quayside*, AC = *car key* or *khaki*.

a. *setter*
b. *restlessness*
c. *Leicester*
d. *Somerset*
e. *handsome*

f. *impersonate*
g. *hamper*
h. *lesson*
i. *restaurant*
j. *perpetuate*

Consider the following questions in your working:

Would you use the same character to represent the first syllable of
handsome and *hamper*, or the first syllable of *impersonate* and *invaluable*?

Would you use the same character to represent the final syllable in both
setter and *Leicester*, or would the middle syllable of *Somerset* be the same
as the final syllable in *setter*?

Would you use two or three characters to write *restaurant*?

Would you use the same character to represent the word *grass* in both
Northern and Southern England, or would you choose two characters
to represent the difference in pronunciation of the same word in the
different areas?

Consider the three different possible ways of saying the plural -*s*, as on
the end of *plates*, *cards* and *thrushes*. How big a saving can be made in
the syllabary if the final syllable of a word can be given an additional
mark to denote 'plural' rather than add to or replace the syllable? Such
marks are termed 'diacritics'. How far could this principle of economy
in the syllabary be taken?

Exploration 6 • *Japanese Syllabaries*

Japanese can be written entirely in one of two 'kana' syllabaries, although
these syllabic characters are normally only used, alongside the ideograms
(kanji) introduced from China, in order to represent particular kinds of words.
Words borrowed from foreign languages are written in katakana characters
(*Figure 10*). Look at the list below of English words that have been imported
into Japanese. In brackets next to each word are indicated the sounds actually
used by the Japanese in pronouncing them. By using these indications find the
characters in *Figure 10* that represent these sounds and write out the words in
the katakana syllabary. (An underlined syllable represents a long vowel.)

1. *tennis* (te - ni - su)
2. *door* (do - a)
3. *test* (te - su - to)
4. *(suit)case* (<u>ke</u> - su)
5. *record* (re - <u>ko</u> - do)
6. *coffee* (<u>ko</u> - <u>hi</u>)
7. *sausage* (<u>so</u> - <u>se</u> - ji)
8. *cheese* (<u>chi</u> - zu)
9. *toast* (<u>to</u> - su -to)
10. *taxi* (ta - ku - <u>shi</u>)
11. *bag* (ba - ggu)
12. *(neck)tie* (ne - ku - ta - i)
13. *Scotch whisky* (su - ko - chchi, u - i - su - <u>ki</u>)
14. *roast beef sandwich* (<u>ro</u> - su - to, <u>bi</u> - fu, sa - n - do - i - chchi)
15. *London* (ro - n - do - n)

(N.B. the Japanese do not distinguish between the sounds 'l' and 'r'.)

ア	カ	ガ	サ	ザ	タ	ダ	ナ	ハ	バ	パ	マ	ラ	ワ	ファ	ン
a	ka	ga	sa	za	ta	da	na	ha	ba	pa	ma	ra	wa	fa	n
イ	キ	ギ	シ	ジ	チ	ヂ	ニ	ヒ	ビ	ピ	ミ	リ		フィ	
i	ki	gi	shi	ji	chi	ji	ni	hi	bi	pi	mi	ri		fi	
ウ	ク	グ	ス	ズ	ツ	ヅ	ヌ	フ	ブ	プ	ム	ル			
u	ku	gu	su	zu	tsu	zu	nu	fu	bu	pu	mu	ru			
エ	ケ	ゲ	セ	ゼ	テ	デ	ネ	ヘ	ベ	ペ	メ	レ		フェ	
e	ke	ge	se	ze	te	de	ne	he	be	pe	me	re		fe	
オ	コ	ゴ	ソ	ゾ	ト	ド	ノ	ホ	ボ	ポ	モ	ロ		フォ	ヲ
o	ko	go	so	zo	to	do	no	ho	bo	po	mo	ro		fo	o
ヤ	キャ	ギャ	シャ	ジャ	チャ	ヂャ	ニャ	ヒャ	ビャ	ピャ	ミャ	リャ			
ya	kya	gya	sha	ja	cha	ja	nya	hya	bya	pya	mya	rya			
ユ	キュ	ギュ	シュ	ジュ	チュ	ヂュ	ニュ	ヒュ	ビュ	ピュ	ミュ	リュ			
yu	kyu	gyu	shu	ju	chu	ju	nyu	hyu	byu	pyu	myu	ryu			
ヨ	キョ	ギョ	ショ	ジョ	チョ	ヂョ	ニョ	ヒョ	ビョ	ピョ	ミョ	リョ			
yo	kyo	gyo	sho	jo	cho	jo	nyo	hyo	byo	pyo	myo	ryo			

Figure 10

Exploration 7 • *One Sound One Character: the Phoneme*

The inhabitants of the Canaanite region at the Eastern end of the Mediterranean simplified the process of writing during the second millennium BC. They abandoned the logographic concept and used only a syllabic form of writing. In the structure of their Semitic language, as in modern Arabic or Hebrew, the essential sound of a syllable was conveyed by consonants, vowels playing a less important role. As a result the syllabic system of writing evolved into an alphabetic one, composed of 22 signs representing consonants. When the Greeks adapted this alphabet to write their own language, they added characters to represent vowels sounds; the absence of vowel sound indicators in Greek would have been too confusing. In doing this, the Greeks reached the idea of a phonemic system of writing, where each character of the alphabet stands for a distinctive unit of sound (a phoneme). The two main alphabets of Europe – the Latin (as used in English) and the Cyrillic (as used in Russian) – were derived in turn from the Greek.

Task | Look at the Russian version of the Cyrillic alphabet in *Figure 11* and work out what the following words of Russian mean in English. The meaning will become apparent as you replace the Cyrillic letters with Latin ones.

a. ВОДКА	d. ФУТБОЛ	g. ЛИФТ	j. БАГАЖ
b. КИЛО	e. ТРАНСПОРТ	h. ГИТАРА	
c. КАНАЛ	f. ТЕЛЕФОН	i. ТАКСИ	

Russian alphabet	English transliteration	Russian alphabet	English transliteration	Russian alphabet	English transliteration
a	a	л	l	ц	c *or* ts
б	b	м	m	ч	č *or* ch
в	v	н	n	ш	š *or* ch
г	g	о	o	щ	šč *or* shch
д	d	п	p	ъ	" *or* "
e (ё)	e (ё)	р	r	ы	y
ж	ž *or* zh	с	s	ь	' *or* '
з	z	т	t	э	ė *or* é
и	i	у	u	ю	ju *or* yu
й	j *or* ĭ	ф	f	я	ja *or* ya
к	k	х	h *or* kh		

Figure 11

Further Exploration

Investigate the Runic alphabet. This alphabet was developed in Germanic
Europe around the third century AD and came to Britain with the Anglo-Saxon
invaders. Its English adaptation had 31 letters and is called the futhorc after the
first six of them.

Further Reading

Runes, R. W. V. Elliott, Manchester University Press, 1959.

Task | Look at the following words of Welsh. Each word closely resembles its
English equivalent in sound. There are no silent letters in Welsh. What
do these words mean?

a. *ambiwlans* f. *drwm* k. *bôl* p. *drôr*
b. *coffi* g. *tacsi* l. *fôt* q. *beic*
c. *nofel* h. *niwclear* m. *bwced* r. *tebot*
d. *plismon* i. *potel* n. *siop* s. *sioc*
e. *ffilm* j. *sinema* o. *siwgr* t. *snwcr*

The following words of Welsh sound akin to their French equivalents.
What do they mean?

a. *llyfr* f. *fflam*
b. *ffenestr* g. *fferm*
c. *duw* h. *mil*
d. *eglwys* i. *aur*
e. *pont* j. *mur*

Consider the following points in your working:

  i. What sound is represented by the letter *c*?
 ii. What sound is represented by the letter *f*?
iii. What sound is represented by the letter *w*?
 iv. How does Welsh represent the sound normally written *sh* in
     English?
  v. How does Welsh represent the sound normally written *f* in
     English?
 vi. What sound is represented by the letter *s*?
vii. What is the function of the diacritic ^ ?
viii. On the basis of the above, how would you expect the following to
     be spelt in Welsh: *cigarette, fork, golf, bus, lamp, sure, active, vandal,
     celery*. (The Welsh words closely resemble their English equivalents
     in sound.)

Exploration 8 • *The English Alphabet*

Is the English alphabet a phonemic alphabet? When you look at words like *bed*, *get*, *bet*, *beg*, you can see a regular correspondence between sounds and the symbols used to represent these sounds. But what about words like the following:

to, too, two

and:

shoot, the, gnaw

and:

cough, rough, though, bough, thorough, hiccough.

Whatever may have been the case in the past, English no longer has a direct correspondence between sounds and spelling. To represent English sounds phonemically we need a special alphabet – a phonetic alphabet.

Exploration 9 • *Alphabets and Codes*

Special alphabets have been developed in response to special needs. Braille was developed for blind people, to take advantage of their sense of touch; morse can convey language by sound in circumstances where speech is impossible; morse can also, like semaphore, convey language through the sense of sight when normal written characters are not useable.

However, in the interests of speedier communication, such alphabets are frequently supplemented by ideograms for ideas that commonly occur. For example the seamen's international code of signalling by flag has a blue flag with a white central rectangle that represents the letter 'p', but when flown on its own at the foremast head in harbour it means that the boat is about to sail. In fact the idea of such supplementary ideograms is not restricted to specialised alphabets. The signs $ for 'dollar' and % for 'percent' are ideograms in general everyday use.

Task | If you look at the semaphore alphabet in *Figure 12* you will see that the badge of the United Kingdom's Campaign for Nuclear Disarmament is composed of a stylised form of the semaphore letters *N* and *D*. Work out comparable logos for the following: USA, River Exe Angling Club, Rio Tinto Zinc, Lake Windermere Sailing Club, The National Theatre. Would any of these logos present difficulties because a flag is in the same position for more than one letter?

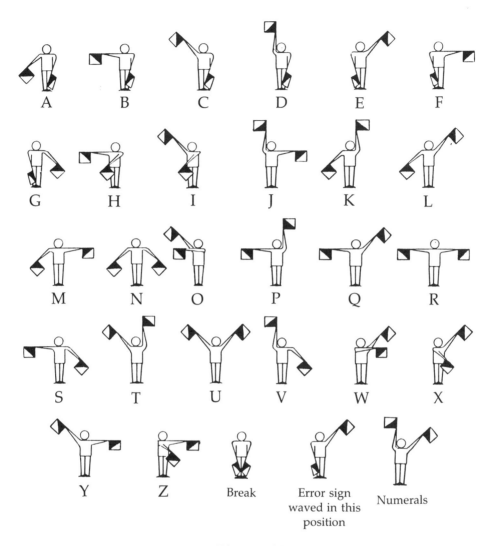

Figure 12

Task Look at the morse code in *Figure 13* and then transmit the following
messages by means of it.
  a. The train has arrived.
  b. We sent two men yesterday.
  c. Martin does not leave until tomorrow.
  d. I have not received your message.
  e. We need help urgently.
  f. Congratulations on winning.

A ·—   N —·

B —···   O ———

C —·—·   P ·——·

D —··   Q ——·—

E ·   R ·—·

F ··—·   S ···

G ——·   T —

H ····   U ··—

I ··   V ···—

J ·———   W ·——

K —·—   X —··—

L ·—··   Y —·——

M ——   Z ——··

Figure 13

Task Look at the characters of the braille system in *Figure 14* and compose the following expressions in them.

a. popular music   d. water rates

b. happy birthday   e. now and then

c. yesterday's paper   f. imported butter

A	B	C	D	E	F	G	H

I	J	K	L	M	N	O	P

Q	R	S	T	U	V	W	X

Y	Z	and	for	of	the	with

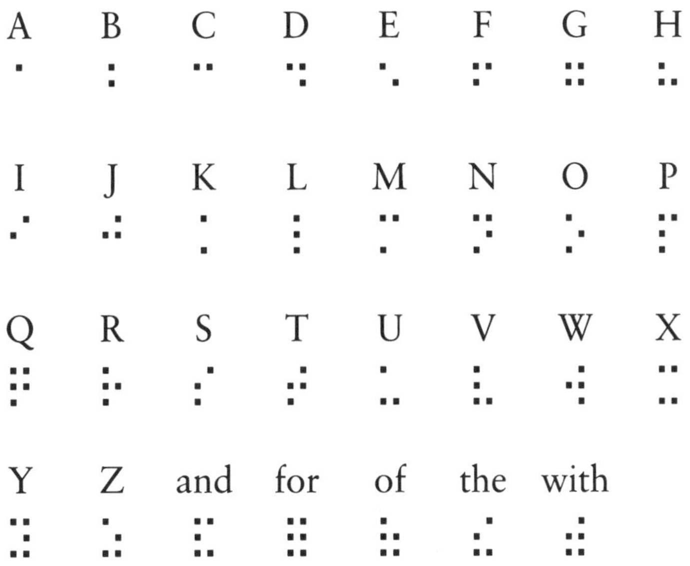

Figure 14

Braille, morse and semaphore are a different kind of alphabet, in that they represent the letters of another alphabet, rather than sounds directly. This is why they are not really alphabets in the sense in which we have been using the term, but rather they are codes.

Further Exploration

Those wishing to know more about the Braille System should contact: Royal National Institute for the Blind, 224-6-8 Great Portland Street, London W1N 6AA.

45

6 *The Sounds of English*

We have seen in Chapters 2 to 5 that language is only one means of communication, and that language itself can have several 'substances'. We have looked at the similarities and differences between language and other communication systems. And we have considered various means of analysing and describing these different ways of communicating.

Now we turn our attention to the description of English, the most widely-used language in the world. We start with the sounds of English – but which English?

Language is not synonymous with communication. Human beings can communicate with one another without the use of language. Human language is not synonymous with speech. If that were the case, anyone unable to speak would be incapable of using language. However, speech is the natural means of conveying language. We learn to speak as part of the process of growing up; other means of conveying language have to be learned by conscious effort and application.

Within each particular language there are variations of use based on geographical region, social class, social activity or social relationships. A range of such variations can be combined in one native speaker, who in addition can vary his or her use of the language according to the role and the degree of formality to be adopted at any given moment. We can take this idea of variation even further, because, if we examined the language use of every native speaker closely enough, we would find that it contained clear, albeit small, differences from the next person's command of the same regional or social variations in the language.

The notion of variations of use within a language has to be balanced against the function of language as a means of communication. The native speaker has individual variations in his or her use of the language, but these are held in check by the need to be understood. Likewise contact between different regional and social variations leads to the development of a standard form alongside those varieties. Universal education and mass communications consolidate such standard forms.

Exploration 1 • *The Sounds of RP English*

Standard British English is frequently, but not necessarily, transmitted in the accent known as Received Pronunciation – RP for short. RP represents the pronunciation of the South East of England. It has also been called at various times 'Queen's English', 'BBC English' and 'Public School English'. It is often considered to be an accent of some prestige, though this is diminishing.

It is possible to speak Standard English in a regional accent, and indeed most people do. It is also possible to speak a regional dialect in RP, though this is very unlikely.

We use RP in this discussion of the sounds of English because it is well documented, and because it is generally understood. It is with the sounds of RP that we begin exploring the sounds of English and of speech in general.

If we wish to represent the sounds of speech unambiguously on paper, we need a special set of characters based on the phonemic principle, with one character corresponding to one unit of sound. The set of characters used here to represent the sounds of RP English are based on the International Phonetic Alphabet (IPA) as used by Professor A. C. Gimson in his *Introduction to the Pronunciation of English*, Arnold, 1980. To avoid confusion between letters of normal spelling and phonemic characters it is customary to write the latter between oblique lines thus: /t/, /u:/.

Look at the list of phonemic characters below. Alongside each one are words that contain (underlined) the sound it represents. Remember that we are representing sounds and not letters or spelling. The sounds are grouped together under consonants, single vowels and diphthongs.

Consonants

/p/   pin nip apple proof hiccough imply
/b/   big rib scribble bring amber trouble
/t/   tip pit hated caught Thomas rushed
/d/   dog bud cuddle prayed folded dado
/k/   kind cold charisma gymkhana queue except back club
/g/   game rag exhaust signify hamburger
/m/   mean team lamb solemn amount amnesty
/n/   north happen plunder knit gnome mnemonic foreign
/ŋ/   wing angry singer bank anxious handkerchief
/f/   feel sniff anglophile cough free wife
/v/   very leave river valves revive version
/θ/   thin path through mathematics wreath throw
/ð/   there although neither the then bathe
/s/   sweet place sets pseudo blessing scythe circle

/z/   <u>z</u>oo bu<u>g</u>s sci<u>ss</u>or<u>s</u> <u>z</u>erox rai<u>s</u>e de<u>s</u>ign ob<u>s</u>erve
/ʃ/   <u>sh</u>ip ru<u>sh</u> mi<u>ss</u>ion <u>s</u>ugar ra<u>t</u>ion ma<u>ch</u>ine
/ʒ/   lei<u>s</u>ure ca<u>s</u>ual deri<u>s</u>ion a<u>z</u>ure
/tʃ/   <u>ch</u>ild mu<u>ch</u> tha<u>tch</u> ri<u>t</u>ual righ<u>t</u>eous <u>t</u>une
/dʒ/   <u>j</u>unk <u>g</u>erm we<u>dg</u>e ma<u>g</u>ic sand<u>w</u>i<u>ch</u> nu<u>dg</u>ed
/r/   <u>r</u>ip me<u>rr</u>y <u>g</u>rant <u>t</u>ramp
/l/   <u>l</u>amp medd<u>l</u>e mi<u>l</u>k e<u>l</u>ephant wastefu<u>l</u> exce<u>ll</u>ent
/w/   <u>w</u>ax q<u>u</u>iet t<u>w</u>in mo<u>w</u>er <u>wh</u>ich lang<u>u</u>age
/j/   <u>y</u>ou <u>y</u>es be<u>au</u>ty d<u>e</u>w <u>u</u>nion
/h/   <u>h</u>elp <u>wh</u>ose be<u>h</u>ave re<u>h</u>eat

Vowels (the diacritic ː indicates that the vowel is lengthened)
/iː/   f<u>ee</u>t m<u>ea</u>t w<u>e</u> p<u>eo</u>ple bel<u>ie</u>ve concr<u>e</u>te
/ɪ/   f<u>i</u>t wr<u>i</u>tten b<u>u</u>sy pr<u>e</u>tty w<u>o</u>men rel<u>i</u>c
/e/   b<u>e</u>d s<u>ai</u>d w<u>ea</u>ther bl<u>e</u>mish surr<u>e</u>nder Th<u>a</u>mes
/æ/   b<u>a</u>d l<u>a</u>ck fr<u>a</u>ntic p<u>a</u>ssion c<u>a</u>n-c<u>a</u>n <u>a</u>ngry
/ɑː/   c<u>a</u>r f<u>a</u>ther p<u>a</u>rt h<u>a</u>lf <u>a</u>rtery pl<u>a</u>nt
/ɒ/   h<u>o</u>t y<u>a</u>cht g<u>o</u>ne kn<u>o</u>wledge qu<u>a</u>lity wh<u>a</u>t
/ɔː/   p<u>o</u>rt b<u>ou</u>ght b<u>o</u>red w<u>a</u>lk <u>au</u>tomatic br<u>oa</u>d
/ʊ/   b<u>oo</u>k w<u>ou</u>ld w<u>o</u>man p<u>u</u>t h<u>oo</u>d w<u>o</u>lf
/uː/   s<u>ui</u>t f<u>oo</u>d pr<u>o</u>ve wh<u>o</u>se thr<u>ou</u>gh tw<u>o</u>
/ʌ/   b<u>u</u>n fl<u>oo</u>d am<u>o</u>ng <u>o</u>ne d<u>oe</u>s r<u>ou</u>gh
/ɜː/   w<u>o</u>rd b<u>i</u>rd l<u>ea</u>rn <u>jo</u>urnal pref<u>e</u>rred c<u>o</u>lonel
/ə/   <u>a</u>lone bett<u>er</u> thor<u>ough</u> ted<u>iou</u>s cupb<u>oar</u>d s<u>u</u>pport

Diphthongs
/eɪ/   r<u>ay</u> w<u>ai</u>t pl<u>a</u>te r<u>a</u>ce
/əʊ/   l<u>oa</u>d gr<u>ow</u> br<u>oo</u>ch bur<u>eau</u>
/aɪ/   h<u>igh</u> fl<u>y</u> b<u>uy</u> b<u>i</u>nd
/aʊ/   br<u>ow</u> b<u>ough</u> d<u>ou</u>bt m<u>ou</u>se
/ɔɪ/   t<u>oy</u> b<u>oi</u>l ann<u>oy</u>ed <u>oy</u>ster
/ɪə/   j<u>ee</u>r f<u>ea</u>r h<u>ere</u> id<u>ea</u>
/ɛə/   h<u>air</u> th<u>ere</u> w<u>ear</u> r<u>are</u>
/ʊə/   m<u>oor</u> s<u>ure</u> t<u>our</u> d<u>our</u> c<u>ure</u>

(The final diphthong provides a good example of change taking place in pronunciation. Younger RP speakers are more likely to prefer /ɔː/ as their vowel in *moor* /mɔː/ and *sure* /ʃɔː/; they tend to be less certain whether to choose /ɔː/ or /ʊə/ in pronouncing *cure* /kjɔː/ or /kjʊə/ and *tour* /tɔː/ or /tʊə/, whereas older RP speakers are more likely to opt for /ʊə/.)

Task | Write down the phonemic character for the first sound in each of the following words:

coat, Philip, centre, jury, knight, think, challenge, Europe, general, awkward, psalm, honest, island, ptarmigan, pneumonia, wrought, practice, their, aeroplane, ahead.

Task | Write down the character for the vowel or diphthong in the RP pronunciation of the following words:

rouse, plane, least, trouble, mien, chose, qualm, goes, troupe, jewel, brawn, curled, taut, plait, won, time, pull, mourn, tracks, all.

Task | Write down the character for the final sound in each of the following words:

gong, little, fetch, linked, takes, pleased, breathe, wife, your, bids, dredge, ewe, hectic, beautifully, banana, gauche, benign, hymn, recipe, blouse.

Task | Rewrite the following words in phonemic characters:

sought, should, proud, through, enough, though, bough, cough, thorough, hiccough, eye, I, aisle, choir, isle, height, dye, iron, white, strait.

Task | Look at the following words. In each case the same spelling has two different pronunciations to which two distinct meanings are attached. They are homographs. Write down in phonemic characters for each spelling two pronunciations that involve a change of meaning: *read, sewer, wound, live, tear, bow, minute, use, tower, lead, singer, pasty, sow, wind, refuse, bass, content, resign, flower, restrain.*

Task | The following list is a phonemic transcription of two homophones: words which are pronounced similarly, but which have a different spelling and meaning. Write down two spellings for each of the following transcribed pronunciations: greɪt, weðə, djuː, siːn, swiːt, sʌn, rəʊd, selz, haɪə, pɔːz, steɪk, raɪt, kiː, peə, piːs, rɪəl.

Task | Within RP, as in other accents, there are words which can be spoken with more than one pronunciation without the meaning being affected by the change. For example, the word *either* can be pronounced /iːðə/ or /aɪðə/, but the listener will understand the same meaning in either case. Look at the following transcriptions of RP pronunciations and write down in phonemic characters a possible alternative that an RP speaker could use when conveying each word.

ɒnvələʊp, trɑːnspɔːt, prɪvəsɪ, gærɑːʒ, sɒvjet, ekənɒmɪks, et, ɒfən, æmætə, buːkeɪ, gleɪsɪə, eɪʒən, əgen, deɪbrɪ

Task | Each of the sentences below contains a major error of transcription. Your accent may not be exactly the same as the speaker's even if you are an RP speaker, but this will not affect your ability to spot these errors.

a. ðə faɪə wəs aʊt
b. ʃʌt ðə dɔː
c. brɪŋ ðə bʊk
d. wɪtʃ wʌn won
e. kʌm bæck leɪtə
f. hiː sɪŋz ɪn ðə kuaɪə
g. ʃiː snɪfd ðə fuːd
h. hiː drəʊve tə taʊn

i. aɪl kɔːl ðə pliːce
j. haʊw menɪ keɪm
k. θeɪ sæt daʊn
l. ɪts maɪ pleʃə
m. biːdz ɑː nestɪŋ ɪn ðə triː
n. lɪsən tə ðə nuːz hedlaɪnz
o. tel hɪm ðə ɑːnsə

Further Reading

An Introduction to the Pronunciation of English, A. C. Gimson, Edward Arnold, 1980 (with tape).
A Practical Course of English Pronunciation, A. C. Gimson, Edward Arnold, 1975.

Exploration 2 • *Regional Accents of English*

Standard British English can be conveyed by accents other than RP. In this Exploration there are some samples of sounds in regional accents of the United Kingdom, where there is a contrast with the equivalent RP pronunciation. The compass of this book can do no more than give an indication that such contrasts exist and, hopefully, that they are no better or worse in themselves as sounds. Suggestions for further reading about regional accents can be found at the end of this Exploration. In the final two parts of the Exploration there is a brief examination of accents of English based beyond the limits of the United Kingdom.

Variations in Accents

Task | The RP diphthong /aʊ/ is realised in different sounds in other accents. Look at the following transcriptions of words containing the equivalent of this diphthong in five English accents. Work out the meaning of each word.

a. (Somerset) kɛy nɛy brɛyn dɛyn
b. (Berkshire) eʉt keʉntə reʉnd deʉn
   (/ʉ/ represents a vowel between /iː/ and /uː/)
c. (Cockney) taːn laːd naː kraːd
d. (Edinburgh) hus dun kutʃ pund
e. (Belfast) klɑyd fɑynd dɑyn ʃɑyt

(N.B. Other realisations of some of these diphthongs are possible.)

One result of the fact that different accents of English have different vowel systems is that two separate vowels in one accent may be pronounced identically in another. This can create homophones in one accent of two words that are pronounced differently in another. The five accents below have homophones in cases where RP makes a distinction, because the single sound symbolised beside the accent's region can convey either of the two sounds of RP symbolised in the adjacent brackets.

a. Norfolk /ɛː/ – (/ɪə/ and /ɛə/)

b. Yorkshire /ʊ/ – (/ʌ/ and /ʊ/)

c. Liverpool /ɜː/ – (/ɛə/ and /ɜː/)

d. Edinburgh /ɔ/ – (/ɒ/ and /ɔː/)

e. Tyneside /ɔː/ – (/ɜː/ and /ɔː/)

Task | With this information work out the different RP pronunciations of each of the following and state which of the above accents is being referred to:

bɛː pʊt tɔt ʃɔːt hɛː
fɜː kɔt fɔːst lʊk bɜːd

Task | Conversely distinctions of pronunciation may be made in regional accents which have been lost or have never existed in RP. Look at the following pairs of words and their pronunciations in each of the five accents below. Then give a transcription for the RP equivalent for each pair.

a. West Midlands *won* /wʊn/; *one* /wɒn/;

b. South Wales: *blew* /blɪu/; *blue* /bluː/;

c. Norfolk: *nose* /nuːz/; *knows* /nɔuz/;

d. Cockney: *bored* /bɔed/; *board* /boːd/;

e. Tyneside: *talk* /taːk/; *torque* /tɔːk/.

London (Cockney)

Task | Look at the following Cockney vowel sounds: /æɪ/ for the vowel in *tape*, /ʌʊ/ for the vowel in *coat*, /ɑɪ/ for the vowel in *like*, /oʊ/ for the vowel in *walk* and /aː/ for the vowel in *town*. Based on this information, transcribe the following words. You may assume that the accompanying consonants are pronounced like their RP counterparts.

talk, rope, found, side, bone, take, flies, pound, caught, make.

Task | It is a feature of the Cockney accent that [θ] and [ð] are frequently realised by [f] and [v] respectively. With this feature in mind:

a. write down the following Cockney pronunciations in their Standard English spellings:

wɪv bæɪv fɪŋk nɑɪvə brʌvə

b. write down two Standard English spellings for each of the following transcriptions of Cockney homophones, which RP and other accents of English distinguish by means of the contrast between [f], [v] and [θ], [ð]:

fɪn fouʔ lɑːvə fɜːst friː

(ʔ represents the glottal stop, which frequently replaces the sound /t/ in some accents of English).

West Midlands

Task In the accent of Birmingham and the West Midlands the following diphthongs are used to express the vowels in the words alongside them: /æɪ/ in *paper*, /ʌʊ/ in *boat*, /ɔi/ in *buy*, /əʊ/ in *food* and /ɑi/ in *bead*. Based on this information transcribe the words below as you think they would be pronounced in a West Midlands accent. You may assume that the consonants are pronounced like their RP equivalents.

try, suit, rain, weed, loaf, mood, why, soap, seed, tame.

Norfolk

Task In the Norfolk accent the sound /j/ is omitted after a consonant. With this feature in mind:

a. write down the following Norfolk pronunciations in Standard English spellings:

tuːn muːzɪk fuː duːrɪn vuːz

b. The following are transcriptions of Norfolk homophones. Write down the two words that each represents. Remember the omission of /j/ after consonants:

duː muːt kuːt huː buːʔɪ

Southern Irish

Task Write out the following transcriptions of words spoken in a typical Southern Irish accent.

kaːr dɪn maʊt̪ feːs kaːm daʊn d̪ɛn keɪr d̪oː t̪ɔːt niːr taɪm feːt̪ boːt plænt taʊn t̪ɪŋk stʌd fʊt ɡʊd bɛd bæt̪

(t̪ and d̪ represent /t/ and /d/ pronounced with the tongue against the top teeth).

General American

There is no accent in the United States of America that is comparable in rôle and status to RP in England. For purposes of comparison here we will take the accent termed General American or Network American and the one usually taught to learners of English as a foreign language. The vowel sounds of this accent (in the same sequence as the RP vowel sounds in 6 Exploration 1) are:

/i/	b<u>ea</u>d tr<u>ee</u>
/ɪ/	b<u>i</u>t st<u>i</u>ff
/ɛ/	b<u>e</u>d p<u>e</u>n
/æ/	b<u>a</u>d c<u>a</u>b
/æ/	gr<u>a</u>ph p<u>a</u>th p<u>a</u>ss
/ɑ/	l<u>o</u>t st<u>o</u>p T<u>o</u>m y<u>a</u>cht p<u>a</u>lm
(/ɑr/	f<u>ar</u> st<u>ar</u>)
/ɔ/	th<u>ou</u>ght cl<u>o</u>th l<u>o</u>st w<u>a</u>lk
(/ɔr/	<u>or</u> f<u>or</u>)
/o/	s<u>oa</u>p d<u>ou</u>gh c<u>oa</u>l r<u>o</u>be
(/or/	p<u>our</u> d<u>oor</u> ad<u>ore</u>)
/ʊ/	f<u>oo</u>t p<u>u</u>sh
/u/	b<u>oo</u>t pr<u>oo</u>f
/ʌ/	b<u>u</u>t r<u>u</u>sh
(/ʌr/	h<u>ur</u>t w<u>or</u>d b<u>ur</u>n c<u>ur</u>se)
/ə/	comm<u>a</u>
(/ɚ/	lett<u>er</u>)
/eɪ/	b<u>a</u>se n<u>a</u>me
/aɪ/	n<u>i</u>ce l<u>i</u>ke
/aʊ/	m<u>ou</u>th n<u>ou</u>n
/ɔɪ/	b<u>oy</u> m<u>oi</u>st
/ɪr/	b<u>eer</u> <u>ear</u> w<u>eir</u>d
/ɛr/	h<u>air</u> p<u>air</u> sh<u>are</u>
/ʊr/	s<u>ure</u> t<u>our</u>

Task | With the help of this list, read the following transcriptions of American pronunciations:

wɛr kɑg pɪrs rom tʃɛrtʃ sɔs wɔr nɑnsɛns ʃæl bɑks krɔl luz paʊdɚ ʃɑrp hɪr kɑm kɔst æftɚ græft dʒɪræf

Further Reading

Accents of English, J. C. Wells, Cambridge University Press, 1982

English Accents and Dialects, Arthur Hughes and Peter Trudgill (second edition), Edward Arnold, 1987.

Listening

Tapes of English accents accompany both the above works.

English with a Dialect, BBC Cassettes, ZCM 173.

7 Stress and Intonation

Now that we have described the individual sounds of English, we can start to look at what happens to those sounds when we start putting them together in words or sentences. Yet again, we find that we communicate a lot more than we 'say'.

Exploration 1 • Stress

In the BBC television series 'To the Manor Born', Penelope Keith played the part of Mrs Audrey fforbes-Hamilton, a firm-minded member of a family of English landed gentry. At one point she corrected the pronunciation of her companion, saying 'It's not /faɪnæns/; it's /fɪnæns/. It's not /riːsɜːtʃ/; it's /rɪsɜːtʃ/.' What she was objecting to was the position of the stress. She was insisting that the words should be pronounced with the stress on the second syllable, not the first.

Stress is an important factor in the pronunciation of English, as it is in other languages like Russian, German and Spanish. In the case of some languages the spelling system includes an indication of where in a polysyllabic word the stress should be placed. For example, the diacritic over the first *a* of *Málaga* indicates that the stress falls on the first syllable, when the name of this Spanish city is pronounced. The spelling system of English does not indicate the position of the stress in a word, so special notation is necessary when discussing it. The one used here indicates stress by placing a short vertical line at the top left of the first letter of the stressed syllable, e.g. /fɪ'næns/, /rɪ's3ːtʃ/.

Task | The following words are pronounced in British English with one syllable stressed. Rewrite the words, indicating the syllable that is stressed.

delay, arrest, position, forty, atomic, extinguish, tomorrow, suggest, maisonette, candidate, method, brewery, prepare, religious, razor, schedule, caterpillar, Italy, garlic, democracy.

Task | The following words change their meaning or use when the stress is transferred from one syllable to another. For example *frequent* /'fri:kwənt/ with the stress on the first syllable means 'repeated at short intervals' and is an adjective, whereas /frɪ'kwent/ with the stress on the second syllable means 'to visit regularly' and is a verb. Work out for each of the following words two meanings which depend on the position of the stress for their contrast.

content, present, object, invite, perfect, recount, conduct, rebel, convict, refuse, subject, contract, reject, exploit, import, project, fragment, insult, entrance.

Exploration 2 • *Primary and Secondary Stress*

The pronunciations of *finance* and *research* which were taboo to Mrs fforbes-Hamilton were stressed on the first syllable, but in addition the second syllable carried some, though less, stress. Words of two or more syllables can carry further stress in addition to their main or primary one. Such stresses are called secondary, not being as prominent as the primary one. For example, compare the stresses on *prophesy* and *prophecy*. The verb *prophesy* has secondary stress on the final syllable, in addition to primary stress on the first syllable. The noun *prophecy* has primary stress on the first syllable, but no secondary stress. Secondary stress is conveyed in the notation used here by a short vertical line at the bottom left of the first letter of the syllable in question. Therefore the two words *prophesy* and *prophecy* would be marked for stress thus: /'prɒfɪˌsaɪ/ and /'prɒfəsɪ/.

Task | The following words are normally pronounced in British English with both a primary and a secondary stress. Rewrite the words, putting primary and secondary stress marks in front of the appropriate syllables.

assimilate, education, helicopter, terminological, grapefruit, unpretentious, armchair, independence, pronunciation, centipede, incomprehensible, revolution, uninteresting, humility, privatise, intonation, realign, intercede, realisation, superiority.

Task | British English gives a different stress pattern to the pronunciation of some words compared with that given by American English. The following words fall into that category. The difference in pronunciation may involve a change of the position of the primary stress. It may involve the presence or absence of secondary stress. For example *militarily* would normally be stressed on the first syllable in British English thus: /'mɪlɪtrəlɪ/, whereas in American English the first syllable would have secondary stress with the primary stress on the third syllable thus: /ˌmɪlɪ'tærɪlɪ/. Write out the words twice, marking them for

British English and American English stress patterns. (In working through this exploration it must be borne in mind that individual British English speakers may have adopted an American stress pattern or vice versa.)

refectory, temporarily, detail, laboratory, m(o)ustache, garage, advertisement, formidable, primarily, inquiry, finance, dictionary, jubilee, renaissance, harassment, research, address, vermouth, comparable, massage.

Task The following words have different meanings, depending on their stress patterns. In each case, when the stress pattern changes, the pronunciation of the underlined vowels changes. For each word give two meanings that depend on a change of stress for their contrast and affect the sound of the underlined vowels.

alternate, deliberate, compliment, defile, attribute, associate, separate, invalid, confines, record.

Exploration 3 • *Stress in Sentences*

Mark the stressed syllables in the following sentences.

a. *He heard the dog.*
b. *She upset the dustbin.*
c. *She parked in front of the house.*
d. *The cat sat on the mat.*
e. *Sylvia had broken her arm.*

f. *The dog chased the sheep.*
g. *Mrs Hinkley polished the table.*
h. *Buy me another book.*
i. *The children liked the ice cream.*
j. *They were overtaking a bus.*

Task One particular stressed syllable in a sentence normally attracts the prime attention of the listener. This syllable, the nucleus of the sentence, tends to be the last stressed syllable in the sentence, but the nucleus can be shifted elsewhere for emphasis. What in your opinion will be the position of the nuclear stress in the following sentences? (Imagine these sentences are being said without any special emphasis.)

a. *John is eating a peach.*
b. *She drinks a lot of tea.*
c. *Can I have the salt?*
d. *Put the light out.*
e. *They said it was true.*

f. *We're taking the road to Inverness.*
g. *What's the time?*
h. *It was raining in Devon.*
i. *He got off at the corner.*
j. *Jane didn't phone.*

Exploration 4 • *Stress and Emphasis*

Task | Variations of meaning can be given to a sentence by shifting the nuclear stress. Look at the following sentences. By moving the nuclear stress to as many positions as possible, work out as many different meanings for them as you can.

    a. *That is my favourite niece.*

    b. *I ordered three chocolate ices.*

    c. *What is wrong with selection?*

    d. *I want a bottle of red wine.*

    e. *Grandma broke the blue jug yesterday.*

Exploration 5 • *Voice Pitch*

A recent television commercial for beer had a dialogue consisting entirely of the word *well*, spoken with different tones of voice to convey different meanings. The dialogue is outlined below with, in brackets, an indication of the meaning conveyed by the pitch of the voice in each case.

– 'Well!'   (John, Harry and David meet one another unexpectedly in the pub.)

– 'Well?'   (John asks the others what they want to drink.)

– 'We-ell.' (David can't make up his mind.)

– 'Well.'   (Harry wishes the others 'Good Health'.)

– 'Well!'   (John sees a pretty girl.)

– 'Well!'   (David is surprised to see the others drink so fast.)

– 'Well?'   (But asks them if they want another.)

– 'We-ell.' (Harry hesitates.)

– 'We-ell.' (John indicates 'Why not?')

– 'Well.'   (After the second round they agree it's time to be going and part company.)

Now look at the following six pitch contours commonly used in British English, with suggestions for the implications they can convey. The notation used to describe them in this book is placed on the word *yes* after each one.

– low falling;   factual, detached, straightforward tone; /ˌjes/

– high falling;   tone of liveliness, exclamation, mild surprise; /ˈjes/

– low rising;   tone of incompleteness, calm and quiet warning or exhortation; /ˌjes/

– high rising;   asking, querying tone; /ˈjes/

– falling rising;   tone of hesitation, reservation, grudging admission; /ˇjes/

– rising falling;   impressed or challenging tone; /ˆjes/

Task | Imagine that a TV sports presenter is giving football results live to the camera as they come through on a teleprinter. Suggest the intonation that might be given to the pronunciation of the ten numbers in the following scores, bearing in mind the circumstances stated in the brackets.

a. *Goole 0   Barry 0*

(The presenter thinks this a dull, inconclusive result between two uninteresting teams.)

b. *Arsenal 1   Peterborough 2*

(A very surprising away win.)

c. *Torquay 1   Southampton 3*

(There is a long pause on the teleprinter after the Torquay score is given and at half-time Torquay were holding a shock lead.)

d. *Halifax 3   Ipswich 0*

(The presenter thinks this is an incredible result that perhaps ought to be checked.)

e. *Newcastle 2   Crewe 0*

(This is an uneventful win that the presenter feels was to be expected.)

Exploration 6 • *Stress, Pitch and Meaning*

Task Some languages, e.g. Chinese, use differences in the pitch to make changes in the meaning of a word. Such languages are known as tone languages. Change of pitch does not affect meaning in English in this way; it affects the way in which a group of words is meant to be understood. Look at the following sentences with pitch and stress markings added and suggest a context in which they might have been spoken. (The primary stress mark on the nuclear syllable is replaced by the appropriate pitch marking.)

a. *I 'think she is delightful!*

b. *'Seven 'sevens are 'forty éight?*

c. *He 'came on his bicycle.*

d. *'Please don't worry.*

e. *There's 'nothing 'wrong at all.*

f. *She's pretty.*

g. *What a ,week-,end!*

h. *We 'got your 'card alright.*

i. *You 'said what?*

j. *\Up to a point ,Lord ,Copper.*

(Note in the last example that the pre-nuclear stress is marked with ↘. This is to indicate the sliding effect of the sounds preceding the nucleus. This sliding, rather than stepping, effect is usually found in the context of a falling-rising or a rising-falling pitch pattern.)

Task | In the above sentences, how are question and exclamation marks used to reflect the pitch patterns?

Task | Look at the sentences in Exploration 4. In addition to moving the nuclear stress to as many positions as possible, see how many pitch patterns could fit plausibly in each of these positions. How many further variations of meaning can be obtained for the sentences as a result?

Exploration 7 • *Pausing for Sense: Tone Groups*

The sentences in Exploration 6 were short and could be spoken without any break or pause. In longer sentences the sense will often call for a break, which will be marked by a small pause in the delivery. Such pauses would not be as marked as those coming at major breaks in the sense, as at the end of a sentence, and it is usual to distinguish between such major and minor sense groups by closing the end of a minor sense (or tone) group in a piece of speech with a single vertical dividing line and the end of a major group with double vertical lines, as in the sentence: '*If you do that again,| I'll tell your father.||*'

Task | How long a tone group is depends on the speed of delivery. How a sequence of speech is split up into tone groups also depends on the way it is delivered. Look at the following sentences. No indication is given where the pauses, if any, should come in them. Mark in where you consider the pauses should occur and whether there is more than one possible interpretation of the sentence, depending on the location of those pauses. To what extent would your interpretations be reflected in the punctuation?

    a. *Her performance was impressive even if you don't take into account the fact that she has a bad ankle.*

    b. *It seems from what I gather to be one of those simple cases which are extremely difficult.*

    c. *If at first you don't succeed try try try again.*

    d. *Join us after the break when we have the latest on the John Smith affair.*

    e. *We must have lunch sometime but not tomorrow.*

    f. *The incident at Gravesend is a good example of what will happen if improvements are not made by next summer at the latest.*

g. *Your electric mixer wouldn't work properly so I beat the mixture by hand.*
h. *What are you doing Anne asked Jane.*
i. *What he tells has never happened but because he has experienced it in his imagination it is true reality for him.*
j. *It was and I said not but.*

Further Exploration

Collect examples for your *Data Book* where the intonation or stress have made a crucial difference in the meaning.

Collect examples of intonation and stress used in TV commercials.

Further Reading

A Practical Course of English Pronunciation, A. C. Gimson, Edward Arnold, 1975 (with tape or cassette).

Intonation of Colloquial English, J. D. O'Connor and G. F. Arnold, Longman, 1973 (with tape).

8 *Word Structure*

This is where we turn our attention to the grammar of English. We begin by looking at words. What are words made up of? Does it make sense to talk about the structure of words? Are there rules governing new words?

Exploration 1 • *Units of Meaning – Morphemes*

The film tycoon Sam Goldwyn was celebrated for making remarks that appear illogical on first hearing, but which, upon reflection, make sense. He made one of his most famous 'Goldwynisms' when rejecting a proposition on one occasion: '*In two words: im-possible.*' Our first reaction tells us that *impossible* is one word in English and yet with a moment's thought we can agree there are two distinct units of meaning in that word. The prefix *im-* (a variant of the negative prefix *in-*) brings an additional element of meaning when attached to the word *possible*.

Task | Look at the following words and work out how many units of meaning (morphemes) each one contains. If the word is a combination of more than one morpheme, state whether the units can be used as words in their own right (free morphemes) or whether they have to be used with another morpheme, e.g. prefixes, suffixes, plural inflections *-s*, past tense inflections *-ed* (bound morphemes):

chairs, waited, pancake, recall, joyful, prejudge, debriefing, weaknesses, bricklayer, disappearance, minicabs, rewind, lightening, feverishly, algebraic, foreign, unthinkable, unmindful, income.

Exploration 2 • *Prefixes and Suffixes*

Task | Look at the following prefixes and suffixes (together known as affixes). Give a definition for each one and consider whether the affix could be used to create many new words, as for example in Lewis Carroll's use of *un-* to coin the word *unbirthday* (in which case we say it is productive), or whether it is restricted to combination with a fixed number of words, that will not increase, for example *be-* in *bemoan* (unproductive):

ante-, mis-, en-, mini-, pre-, -ful, -less, -ise, hyper-, mega-, re-, pro-, -er, -ly, a-, auto-, anti-, -ment, -hood, pseudo-.

Task How many of these prefixes and suffixes can be used as words in their own right? When they are used as words do they have a connection in meaning with their use as prefix or suffix?

Task How many of these definitions require a description of the use of the prefix or suffix, as opposed to a more traditional dictionary type statement of content or lexical meaning? For example *-ness* will require a definition that involves a description of function: 'is added to adjectives or participles to indicate the state or condition of being X', whereas *sub-* can be glossed as 'under, beneath, lower than'.

Exploration 3 • *Same Affix – Different Form*

Task Consider how the negating prefix *in-* is pronounced in front of the following words and write out the resulting combinations in phonemic script:

prudent, balance, regular, animate, elastic, perfect, liberal, material, plausible, legal.

Task Consider the different forms of the suffix *-tion* when it is used with the following verbs to form nouns, and write out the resulting combinations in both alphabetic and phonemic characters:

intend, assume, decide, invite, confuse, reflect, corrupt, include, revise, promote.

Exploration 4 • *Forgotten Forms*

The identification of morphemes in a word is complicated both by the changing nature of language and by the importing of foreign words. Words like *kempt* have died out in standard English usage, leaving *un-* plus *kempt* as one unit *unkempt*; words like *daisy* have ceased to be thought of as combinations of smaller units ('day's eye') and appear now as irreducible; imported words like *denim* (French 'de Nîmes') enter the language as a free morpheme, without the English speaker being aware that their etymologies reveal combinations of smaller units of meaning.

Task Use a dictionary to discover the etymologies of the following words. Were they single free morphemes in their original language, or were they composed of more than one morpheme?

whisky, gospel, coleslaw, tawdry, cockroach, lord, chauffeur, coxswain, panorama, brunette.

Exploration 5 • *Problems for Analysis*

Task | Look at the following words, which all begin with the letters *re-*. Which of the four categories below applies to each word?

remember, reassess, recreate, reduce, reinvent, resume, reverse, revisit, re-educate, regal, reintroduce, remit, report, repeat, repudiate, resemble, resin, reference, rectangle, reason.

a. When *re-* is removed, we may have a word like (*re-*)*think*, an English free morpheme. Here *re-* is a prefix meaning 'again'.

b. We may have a word like (*re-*)*ject*, where the *re-* looks like the English prefix for 'back, away' (as in *retrace*), yet its removal leaves a non-existent word of English.

c. We may have a word like (*re-*)*tire* where the removal of what looks like the prefix *re-* does leave a word of English (*tire*), but one that has no link of meaning with *retire*.

d. A word beginning with *re-* may not have a prefix at all, as for example *regent*, *reel*, the same spelling being a coincidence.

Exploration 6 • *Regular and Irregular Inflections*

English makes use of a number of inflections (or inflectional affixes), to mark things like the plural of nouns: *car – cars*, the past tense of verbs: *look – looked*, and the comparative of adjectives: *small – smaller*.

These are regular inflections that are very productive. They are sometimes, however, replaced by irregular forms, as for example *drive – drove*, or invariable forms, e.g. *deer – deer*.

Task | Look at the following words, all of which are either irregular or invariable forms of the plural, past tense or the comparative. State the singular, present tense or the positive form of each word. What suffix would it have, if it weren't irregular or invariable?

lice, read, sheep, went, found, better, geese, criteria, taught, was.

Exploration 7 • *Suffixes and Word Class*

Task | Look at the following suffixes. Each one, when added to a word used as one word class (noun, verb, adjective or adverb) derives a different one from it. This is why they are called derivational affixes. For example, *-ness* is added to an adjective and derives a noun (*fond – fondness*). State which word classes the following can be added to, and which one results from the combination:

-ful, -ise, -ment, -ify, -ity, -ish, -able, -dom, -ical, -ly.

Exploration 8 • *New Affixes*

The prefix *mini-* became prominent in the English language in 1959 when the original version of the Mini car was launched by the then British Motor Corporation. The version of the car made in the Cowley works was called the Mini-Minor in reference to the Morris Minor car made at the same factory. However, this version and the Austin counterpart were quickly christened *Mini* by the public and from that the word went on to be used as a prefix meaning 'small', as in *miniskirt*.

Task | Look at the following affixes, which have all come into the language or developed an extended meaning in recent times. Give a meaning definition for each one. Are there any which you do not recognise or which you feel are old-fashioned? Find further examples of those you do recognise.

a. *-sville* (as in 'They played the piece to hackneysville')
b. *-mania* (as in *Beatlemania*)
c. *-ette* (as in *laundrette, dinette*)
d. *-burger* (as in *cheeseburger*)
e. *-(t)eria* (as in *washeteria, cafeteria*)
f. *-wise* (as in *workwise*, 'What's it doing weatherwise?')

Exploration 9 • *Backformations*

Some of the examples in Exploration 8 have developed by false analogy. The chopped meat rissole in a bun known as a *hamburger* got its name through the German suffix *-er* being attached to the name of the city of *Hamburg*. In the same way a certain type of sausage is known as a *frankfurter* by the attachment of this suffix to *Frankfurt*, its traditional home. However, when the *hamburger* was imported into the English-speaking world, the idea developed that *-burger* was the suffix, meaning 'ham, cheese or any other kind of food in a bun', hence *cheeseburger*.

A similar language development takes place in the case of backformations. Backformations involve the removal, through false analogy, of what is mistakenly supposed to be an affix, in order to form another word. This is often used for humorous reasons, for example *to ush* from *usher*, *to buttle* from *butler*, *gruntled* from *disgruntled*, *to misle* from *misled*.

Task | The following words have all given rise to backformations that are now common words of English. Which word do you think was formed in each case? What was the supposed affix that was removed by false analogy?

television, commuter, peevish, burglar, grovelling, pease, enthusiasm, editor, jelly, sherris (wine).

Exploration 10 • *Compound Words*

We have concentrated up to now on the attachment of prefixes and suffixes to words. Free-standing words (free morphemes) also combine with each other to produce compounds like *woodpecker, overtake, outstanding, upstairs*.

Task | Look at the following pairings of compound words and the component words of the compound spelt separately. The difference in meaning between the compound and the two separate words is conveyed in speech by a difference in the stress pattern:

a green house – a greenhouse, a black bird – a blackbird, a paper back – a paperback, a cross word – a crossword, a strong box – a strongbox, a tall boy – a tallboy, a loud speaker – a loudspeaker, a gentle man – a gentleman, a long bow – a longbow, a red cap – a redcap.

Task | The following compounds still retain the recognisable spelling of the component words, but the pronunciations have changed. Rewrite these words in phonemic characters as you would pronounce them. How many of them in your usage have reacquired a pronunciation to fit the spelling?

forehead, cupboard, waistcoat, breakfast, Christmas, halfpenny.

Task | The following words are compounds that have changed in both spelling and pronunciation. By consulting an etymological dictionary discover their original components.

nostril, nickname, sheriff, garlic, gossip, woman.

Exploration 11 • *Hyphenated Words*

We saw in Exploration 10 that words combine to make compounds which in turn enlarge the stock of lexical items. Some compounds are hyphenated, such as *pig-headed, teach-in, baby-sitter,* and there are some groups of words, like *red tape, test drive, hot dog,* which are regarded as one lexical item, even though the component words are normally written separately.

Task | Look at the following lexical items with their component words printed separately. Would you write each by joining the words together, by hyphenating them or by leaving them separate?

with the result that, a mother in law, a pick me up, a fire place, a mae west, an at home, an also ran, a breeches buoy, ham fisted, a letter opener

Further Explorations

In colloquial speech people often replace standard words with more colourful expressions, such as *sweet Fanny Adams* for *nothing* and *kick the bucket* for *die.* Make a note in your *Data Book* of any such expression you come across that is new to you and that you find particularly striking.

Make a note in your *Data Book* of any creative use of word structure that you come across, for example *'My friend Richard says I'm feckless. Well, all I can say is, if you lack feck, you lack feck.'* or *'The Council at Woonsocket, Rhode Island, voted to refer to manholes in future as "person-holes".'*

This last use is an interesting example of how, only quite recently, people have become aware of how language can be used in a sexist way: *man* can mean 'both men and women', but *woman* can't; we tend to use *he* to refer to both men and women; *doctor* doesn't 'mean' 'male doctor', but why then do we find the expression *lady doctor* (not usually *woman doctor*)? Is language sexist, or is our use of it sexist? Collect examples for your *Data Book* and see what conclusions you can draw from them.

In rhyming slang the standard word is replaced by an expression that rhymes with it. Investigate this particular form of colloquial speech.

Introductory reading

Rhyming Cockney Slang, edited by Jack Jones, Abson Books, 1971.
A Dictionary of Rhyming Slang, Julian Franklyn, Routledge and Kegan Paul, 1960.

9 *Word Classes – Nouns*

Words themselves do different things in a sentence. In Chapters 9 to 12 we look at four types of word.

Some words are nouns. What does this mean? Are all nouns the same? What can we do with nouns?

Exploration 1 • *Proper and Common*

There are variations in the way nouns are used. The words *Christopher, cider,* and *chair* are all nouns, but they have differences in their grammatical context. The word *Christopher* will appear without *a, the* or *some* in its normal use, whereas *cider* appears with *the* or *some,* but only with *a* if we are classifying a type of cider; *chair* on the other hand will appear with *the* or *a,* but only with *some* in its plural form in normal usage.

Task | When considering the noun *Christopher* and the fact that it was not preceded by *a* or *the* in normal usage, we were in fact considering a proper noun. A proper noun has unique reference in our minds, unlike a common noun, which refers to one member of a large set. The proper noun refers to a particular person or place, for example, so that further words of definition like the indefinite or definite articles (*a/an, the*) are not required. Look at the following list. Which are proper nouns and which are common nouns?

John, book, Turk, bed, Bath, president, martin, cardigan, Portuguese, Rose.

However the division between proper nouns and common nouns is not as clear-cut as has been implied above. There are proper nouns which were originally common nouns but which have acquired unique reference, for example *The Netherlands, The Wash, The Bible.* Further, when we concentrate on one aspect of a proper noun, we will qualify it with articles and adjectives as if it were a common noun, for example *the older Dickens, the first Christmas, a wet Paris, the London of the 1930s, the Danish Molière.* Indeed there are some common nouns liable to be used with unique reference, such as *the sun, the moon,* and in fact other common nouns can acquire unique reference in particular usage, as *the garden* in *We spent the whole afternoon at home in the garden.*

Task | Look at the following words. They are all common nouns derived from proper nouns and meaning an embodiment of the qualities that made the original famous. What is the meaning of each one and who was the original?

a judas, a quisling, a dunce, a doubting Thomas, a Don Juan, a boycott, a man Friday, an abigail, a Mrs Grundy.

These expressions are examples of one kind of antonomasia. Another aspect of this figure of speech is the substitution of the proper noun by a descriptive expression that retains the unique reference. For example *the Apostle of the Gentiles (St Paul), the Iron Lady (Mrs Thatcher), the First Gentleman of Europe (the Prince Regent), the Athens of the North (Edinburgh), the Eternal City (Rome).*

Further Exploration

Note in your *Data Book* further examples of proper nouns being treated in the ways outlined above.

Exploration 2 • *Mass and Count*

Common nouns can be sub-divided into mass (or non-count) and count nouns. For example the noun *glass* can refer to a hard, siliceous substance, usually transparent, or to a drinking vessel made of that substance. In the former meaning the word is a mass noun and in the latter it is a count noun. A count noun can appear with the indefinite article (*a/an*) and can occur in the plural. The word *some* will occur with a mass noun (*some glass*), but with a count noun only in the plural (*some glasses*). It might be objected that one can refer to *a* (specific kind of) *glass* as in the expression *a high quality plate glass*, but in doing so, the speaker is no longer using the word as a mass noun. The word is being used as a count noun in the same way that saying *a* (kind of) *cheese*, *a* (glass of) *wine*, *a* (pat of) *butter* turns those mass nouns into count nouns. Conversely it is possible for a count noun to be treated as a mass noun, for example in referring to *some pork* as *some pig*.

Task | Look at the following nouns. Which ones strike you as mass nouns and which as count nouns?

beef, knife, custard, snow, head, remark, bus, cup, loaf, book.

Task | Each of the following nouns has distinct, though related meanings, depending on whether it is used as a mass noun or a count noun. Identify those meanings. (Leave aside such possibilities as *a wood* meaning 'a kind of timber'.)

pepper, television, licence, cold, air, paper, gum, corn, shade, football.

Task | Which of the following words or expressions are used to qualify a count noun, which to qualify a mass noun and which can be used with either? In the latter case is there any difference in the context in which the word or expression is used?

enough, much, less, those, either, each, my, (a) few, (a) little, several.

Exploration 3 • *Human, Animate and Inanimate*

Nouns can also be divided into animate or inanimate with a further division of animate into human and non-human. Although these distinctions are based on the lexical meaning of the noun, they are also reflected in the words that are acceptable in context with them.

Task | Look at the following sentences containing words that are relevant to the animate–inanimate, human–non-human distinctions (underlined). Which of these underlined words do you find acceptable in the context and which not?

a. *The baby's broken <u>its</u> rattle./The baby's broken <u>his</u> (<u>her</u>) rattle.*
b. *My cat likes <u>its</u> food./My cat likes <u>her</u> food.*
c. *Tiddles is washing <u>her</u> paws./Tiddles is washing <u>its</u> paws.*
d. *The car was old, but <u>she</u> was a good runner.*
e. *He has a narrow boat on <u>which</u> he spends his holidays.*
f. *We have an assistant on <u>whom</u> we rely a great deal.*
g. *He has two daughters <u>who</u> are both married./He has two daughters <u>that</u> are both married.*
h. *The cheque <u>whose</u> arrival I have been relying on still hasn't come.*
i. *I know the man <u>who</u> just caught that bus./I know the man <u>that</u> just caught that bus.*

When an inanimate or non-human noun is given human qualities, the resulting figure of speech is personification. For example, in the common expression *Money talks* the inanimate noun *money* is personified by being credited with the power of speech. In the nursery rhyme *Hey-Diddle-Diddle* the dog is personified by being given the human quality of laughter, while the inanimate dish and spoon are animated in the last line:

The little dog laughed to see such fun
And the dish ran away with the spoon.

Look at the following words.
Are they normally restricted to use with human or animate nouns, or is their use unrestricted?

see, talkative, gasp, thoughtful, sleep, remain, eat, attractive, disappear, call out.

Further Exploration

How has the idea of personification been used by writers over the centuries in their choice of subject matter, e.g. by George Orwell in *Animal Farm*?

Collect examples in your *Data Book* of the use of personification in everyday expressions, e.g. *The situation cries out for action*, or in common rhymes, e.g. *The Owl and the Pussycat*.

The writer John Ruskin coined the term 'pathetic fallacy' for a particular kind of personification in which human qualities and strong human emotions are ascribed to natural phenomena, for example *angry seas, the wind moaned, threatening mountains, a raging torrent, the generous earth*. In collecting examples of both pathetic fallacy and personification in general, consider how much they have become a part of everyday language use.

Exploration 4 • *Collective and Non-collective*

A further division of nouns can be made between collective and non-collective. If we say *The crowd is getting restless*, we are focussing on the crowd as a collective unit; it is followed by the singular form *is* and we would replace *the crowd* with the singular pronoun *it*. If we say *The crowd are getting restless*, we are focussing on the individuals that make up the crowd; the plural form *are* is used and the plural pronoun *they* would be used to replace *the crowd*.

Task | Look at the following nouns. Which ones are collective?

family, friend, youngster, train, police, committee, tramp, government, forest, staff.

Task | The following nouns can all be used in a collective sense, which is different from, although related to, their meaning when used as non-collective nouns. For example *a board* can refer to a flat piece of wood or to a group of people who sit at it to make decisions (*The board has/have decided*). State both meanings for each noun.

bench, ship, office, country, choir, school, newspaper, garage, guard, authority.

The collective meaning of nouns such as *board, guard* and *factory* is the result of metonymy. This figure of speech gives people or objects the name of something closely associated with them. For example *He is a good bat* is a metonym for *He is a good batsman*. Closely allied with metonymy is the figure of speech called synecdoche, in which a part is used to represent the whole. For example *The cost will be $11 a head, He is watching the news on the box* instead of *$11 per person, on the television*.

Further Exploration

Note in your *Data Book* examples in everyday usage of metonymy, e.g.

First Horn wanted for orchestra

Alcoholics Anonymous got him off the bottle

She addressed her remarks to the chair

and of synecdoche, e.g.

He invested in bricks and mortar

She is a first-rate brain

He's bought a new set of wheels to get to work.

Exploration 5 • *Concrete and Abstract*

Our final sub-division of nouns is between concrete and abstract nouns. As their name implies, concrete nouns are names for perceivable phenomena; abstract nouns are not. Abstract nouns can be divided further into those nouns that are located in time or space like *death, rumour, amazement* and those which are outside time and space like *justice* and *reason*.

Task | Abstract nouns are mostly non-count nouns in English. The following abstract nouns can also be used as count nouns, preceded by the indefinite article (*a/an*). State their altered meanings in such usage, leaving aside such possibilities as *a faith* meaning a demonstration of faith.

relation, licence, distinction, grace, beauty, work, terror, charity, highness, generation.

Exploration 6 • *Noun Phrases*

Up to this point we have been considering nouns only in terms of single words. In 8 Exploration 11 we saw that a lexical item could be composed of more than one word, such as *waiting room* or *all-in wrestling*. Such groupings became single lexical items because a lasting link had grown up between the component words. Many of the examples given in 8 Exploration 11 were in fact noun groupings. Sentences can also contain more temporary noun groupings, formed to express the desired meaning of the moment, such as *a pencil, some other person, a tiresome dog, a somewhat delapidated cottage in the country, the ever heartening sight of the rising sun*. Such groupings are termed noun phrases.

Task | Look at the following sentences and identify the noun phrases they contain. They may be of any length from a single word upwards.

a. *The bus conductor was collecting the fares.*
b. *The old dishwasher in our kitchen has broken down at last.*
c. *The man from the gas board came to read the meter.*
d. *The police wish to interview a tall, well-built man with a red beard.*
e. *The hostess served a cold soup consisting of tomatoes, garlic, onions and green peppers.*
f. *The man sitting next to me in the carriage was reading a newspaper several days old.*

Further Exploration

Collect examples of ambiguous sentences, where the ambiguity arises from a noun being used in two different senses. For example:

a. *He is chewing his gum.* (count and mass noun)
b. *Prudence was their guide.* (proper and abstract noun)
c. *She went into the church.* (collective and non-collective noun)
d. *His resolution won the day.* (abstract and count noun)
e. *He likes fish.* (animate and inanimate).

Further Reading

A University Grammar of English, Randolph Quirk and Sidney Greenbaum, Longman, 1973.

A University Grammar of English Workbook, R. A. Close, Longman, 1974.

10 *Word Classes – Verbs*

Some words are verbs. These words can hold a whole sentence together. We can use them not just to refer to different time periods, but also to reflect in quite subtle ways the speaker's attitude about what he or she is saying.

Exploration 1 • *Transitive and Intransitive*

In the sentences

a. *He dropped the ball.*

b. *Every child likes ice cream.*

c. *The neighbours' dog disappeared.*

d. *I write with my left hand.*

the words *dropped, likes, disappeared* and *write* are verbs. A verb can, however, be composed of more than one word. In the sentences

e. *The little boy is eating chocolate.*

f. *Grandma will be coming on Monday.*

g. *We have seen a gnu.*

h. *They will have been travelling over an hour by now.*

the groupings of *is eating, will be coming, have seen* and *will have been travelling* each constitute a verb.

In the sentences above, each verb was preceded by its subject. These subjects took the form of either pronouns (*He, I, We, They*), single nouns (*Grandma*) or noun phrases (*Every child, The neighbours' dog, The little boy*).

Although all of the verbs had a subject, not every one was followed by a direct object. The verb *dropped* was followed by *the ball, likes* by *ice cream, is eating* by *chocolate* and *have seen* by *a gnu*. These are the direct objects of the verbs concerned and verbs that take a direct object are termed transitive verbs. Verbs like *disappear, come* and *travel* that do not take a direct object after them are called intransitive verbs.

Task | Look at the following verbs. Which ones are transitive and which intransitive?

await, arrive, fall, moan, procrastinate, found, seat, queue, go, put.

In the sentence *I write with my left hand* the verb *write* is used without being followed by a direct object, yet every English speaker knows that it can be followed by one, as in *I write letters reluctantly*. Conversely the verb *eat* in *The little boy is eating chocolate* can be used without a direct object, as in *The little boy is eating*.

Many transitive verbs in English are used without a direct object being stated, as in *He is drinking*, when it is not necessary or not possible to specify, for example, what is being drunk, eaten, written. This is an example of ellipsis – the omission of words.

Task | Which of the following transitive verbs can be used in this way and which ones require their direct object to be mentioned explicitly?

ride, forget, bar, choose, smoke, bake, kill, surprise, disguise, deceive.

Task | The following verbs have one meaning when used intransitively and a different, though related, meaning when used transitively. For example, *grow* used intransitively, as in *He is growing fast* means 'to increase in size', whereas when it is used transitively, as in *She is growing radishes*, it means 'to cultivate'. What are intransitive and transitive meanings for these verbs?

return, stand, set, smell, mix, try, leave, sway, reflect, stagger.

Exploration 2 • *Reflexive Verbs*

When the direct object of the verb has the same identity as its subject, the verb is being used reflexively and the object becomes *myself, herself, themselves*, etc. As in the case of some transitive verbs mentioned in 10 Exploration 1 some reflexive verbs can be used with their reflexive pronoun direct object omitted. Others require it to be stated. For example, *He undressed* will be taken as 'He undressed himself' and any other direct object would have been stated, as in *He undressed the victim*. On the other hand *He cut himself* would not be understood if reduced to *He cut*.

Task | Look at the following verbs. Which of them require the reflexive pronoun direct object to be present and which can be used reflexively with the pronoun omitted?

bathe, calm, warm, kill, steady, delude, rest, undress, shave, hide.

Exploration 3 • *Verbs with Particles and Prepositions*

When it was shown in 10 Exploration 1 that verbs could be composed of more than one word, the examples used were all single-word verbs which had developed multi-word forms in those contexts. The original form of the verb, before the addition of inflections or other words, is known as the infinitive of the verb and is often characterised by the word *to* preceding it, as in *to write, to drink, to eat*.

English also possesses verbs composed of two or three words in their infinitive form, as *to look at, to pick up, to turn over, to come away, to ring up, to look up to, to get out of*. These verbs are called phrasal verbs.

The following sentences involving phrasal verbs:

a. *He turned the lights out.*

b. *He turned out the lights.*

c. *He turned them out.*

are all acceptable English, whereas

d. **He turned out them.*

is not. (The asterisk is the conventional sign for marking an unacceptable sentence.) Compare these sentences with a similar set involving 'to look at':

e. *He looked at the lights.*

f. *He looked at them.*

are acceptable, but

g. **He looked the lights at.*

h. **He looked them at.*

are not. The two verbs do not behave in the same way. Whereas *to turn out* can accept a noun object before or after *out*, it can only accept a pronoun object before *out*. In contrast, *to look at* can only accept its object after *at*, whichever form it takes. To distinguish between these two kinds of verb, words like *out* in *to turn out* are termed particles, and words like *at* in *to look at* are viewed as prepositions.

Task | In the following list of phrasal verbs, which ones have a particle as their second word and which ones a preposition?

get up, laugh at, listen to, look for, call on, take out, care for, object to, put down, drag over.

Task | Look at the following list of phrasal verbs with particles and say whether or not they can take a direct object (either stated or omitted, reflexive or otherwise). In the case of a verb having both a transitive and an intransitive use, is there any marked change of meaning between the two?

stand up, fall out, turn up, come down, look out, run up, get out, go in, give in, walk away.

Exploration 4 • *Tense*

We divide our concept of time into past, present and future and we reflect these divisions in English by altering the form of the verb. The resulting tenses convey our view of the time at which the action of the verb took/takes/will take place.

In English tenses can be shown by:

a. inflections, as when -s is added in *he likes,*

b. additional words, as *will* in *she will come,*

c. a combination of both, as *has* and *-ed* in *she has tried,* or

d. some verbs don't change in form, and have to be understood from the context without inflection or additional words, as in *They cut.*

In order to illustrate the idea of tense, let us compare the simple past tense, as in *I played, You waited, She caught, They said, She threw, I swam,* with the present perfect tense, as in *I have played, You've waited, She has caught, They've said, She's thrown, I have swum.*

These two past tenses convey a different view of past time. Whereas the simple past implies that the action of the verb occurred in the past and has come to a finish, the present perfect tense sees the action of the verb beginning in the past, but extending into the present. (It is for that reason that it is called the 'present perfect'.) For example, *He arrived last week* uses the simple past, but *He has just arrived this minute* uses the present perfect. To test the point, reverse the tenses in these two sentences and consider whether you find the result acceptable.

Task | Rewrite the following sentences, changing the infinitive verb form in brackets to either the simple past or the present perfect, as appropriate. In cases where either tense will fit, consider whether there is a distinction of meaning if you use one rather than the other. To what extent do other words and phrases in the sentences, for example *already, since last winter* and *yesterday,* dictate your choice of tense?

a. *He (leave) yesterday.*   f. *I (consider) resigning last week.*

b. *It (not come) yet.*   g. *I (see) him just a moment ago.*

c. *She (visit) us lately.*   h. *I (not work) since last winter.*

d. *It (survive) up to now.*   i. *He (telephone) finally.*

e. *She (tell) me already.*   j. *I (live) in York for six years.*

American English uses the present perfect less than British English and its speakers would find sentences like *She wrote already* and *He arrived just this minute* more acceptable than British English speakers.

There is, however, a difference between the verb tense and time itself. For example, the present tense form of the verb can be used to convey

a. timelessness, as in *The earth revolves around the sun*,

b. the present moment, as in *Pele dribbles round a defender and shoots*,

c. a past happening, as in *At that moment in walks the landlord* and

d. an event in the future, as in *The train arrives in ten minutes*.

Task | Which of these four possibilities is being conveyed by the present tense in the following sentences?

a. *He writes with his left hand.*

b. *When I eventually find out, I will punish the offender.*

c. *I leave for Venice on Monday.*

d. *At which point the whole company bursts out laughing at him.*

e. *I pronounce you man and wife.*

f. *Dickens attacks contemporary social conditions in his novels.*

Exploration 5 • *Aspect*

The verb form can also be used in English to convey aspect. Aspect is the manner in which the action of the verb is viewed or experienced. For example, it can be presented as completed or still in progress or to be understood with emphasis:

a. We can say *He wrote to his mother* and we view the writing as having been completed.

b. We can say *He was writing to his mother* and this time we view the writing as being in progress, irrespective of whether it was completed or not.

c. We can say *He did write to his mother* and we are giving emphatic prominence to the completion of the writing.

When we transfer this pattern to the present, we see that the simple tense form (*He writes to his mother*) conveys timelessness, but the progressive and emphatic forms retain their same force.

Task Rewrite the following sentences, changing the simple verb forms into the comparable progressive ones, e.g. *He will come – He will be coming*. Are any unacceptable sentences produced as a result?

a. *She carried the plates into the kitchen.*
b. *He has waited for two days.*
c. *Dogs always like bones.*
d. *She went to the shops.*
e. *The guards will have searched everywhere.*
f. *Suddenly he remembered her name.*

Although the progressive aspect is commonly associated with the incompleteness of an action, it can also, depending on the lexical meaning of the verb, convey:

a. repetition, as in *She is nodding*,
b. the beginning of a transition, as in *He is dying*, or
c. immediacy of physical sensation, as in *It is hurting*.

In the last case there is little distinction in meaning between the progressive and the simple forms.

Task Look at the following verbs and say whether, when used in the progressive aspect, they convey:

a. incomplete events in progress,
b. repetition of an action,
c. the beginning of a transition, or
d. immediacy of physical sensation.

itch, leave, hit, say, bleed, run, suffer, drive, read, knock.

Exploration 6 • *Dynamic and Stative*

In Exploration 5 you will probably have rejected as unacceptable the use of the progressive form in sentences c., **Dogs are always liking bones*, and f. **Suddenly he was remembering her name*. Both *like* and *remember* are stative verbs, whose meaning does not allow the progressive aspect, as opposed to dynamic verbs like *wait* and *carry*, which do.

Task | Look at the following sentences with the verb in the simple tense form. By changing the verb into the progressive aspect, discover which of the verbs you consider to be dynamic and which stative.

    a. *My brother resembles Dave Allen.*

    b. *I am a Scot.*

    c. *My feet hurt me.*

    d. *She changed her clothes.*

    e. *They nodded their heads in agreement.*

    f. *We need more food.*

Exploration 7 • *Copulas*

Some verbs act as a connecting link between the subject and a following noun or adjective. This type of verb is known as a copula and the most common example is the verb *to be*. Sentences like *Dinner smells good, Ali became a doctor, Wind-surfing looks fun* have a copula verb between the subjects *dinner, Ali* and *wind-surfing* and their complements *good, a doctor* and *fun*. Such sentences establish a direct link between the subject and the complement. They are one and the same thing. What we are in effect saying is that 'dinner is good', 'Ali is a doctor', 'windsurfing is fun'.

Task | Which of the verbs in the following sentences are acting as copulas?

    a. *He felt fine.*

    b. *Miranda turned pale at the thought.*

    c. *Everyone remained calm.*

    d. *She is making a lot of noise.*

    e. *He tasted the wine.* '

    f. *She turned towards me.*

Exploration 8 • *Mood*

A third factor, after tense and aspect, that affects the composition of verbs is mood. Sentences like *The car stopped at the traffic lights* and *He is putting the cat out* are presented as events. The mood of their utterance is one of fact and certainty. This mood can also be given to sentences concerning the future, even though the event has not yet occurred, as in *The plane will land at 9 o'clock tomorrow morning.*

Mood conveys the attitude of the speaker to what is being said. Other moods, such as possibility, obligation, insistence and permission, may also be given to a sentence. The mood may be expressed by other words apart from the verb, for example by an adverb such as *possibly*, but it is likely to be conveyed partly or entirely by the verb, either through its form, as the hypothetical *were* in *If I were you ...*, or by a modal verb, such as *may, ought, must* and *can, I must leave now – I ought to leave now*. A modal verb may, in addition, distinguish between types of modality by having different tenses, such as *can/could/could have, must/must have, may/might/might have*.

Task	Look at the following sentences and state which mood they convey in your opinion, for example, permission, intention, moral obligation, probability. What words are used to convey that mood? Would the stress and intonation of the utterance play a role in conveying mood?

  a. *You ought to be ashamed of yourself.*
  b. *It's no good. I must take my leave.*
  c. *It's a long shot, but it might just work.*
  d. *You could try again, but I'm not hopeful.*
  e. *It's your own fault; you would push that button.*
  f. *It should be ready after all this time.*
  g. *We shall overcome.*
  h. *You might have electrocuted yourself.*
  i. *I was able to get through the bathroom window.*
  j. *I have to admire your impudence.*

Exploration 9 • *To Do*

We saw in Exploration 5 that the use of *do* in a sentence like *I do like your hat* adds emphasis to the meaning of the verb.

Older English used *do* as an auxiliary without any emphatic force, so that *When I do wonder, ...* and *You did send*, for example, had the same force as *When I wonder, ...* and *You sent*.

The verb *do* is still used as an auxiliary without emphatic force in questions and negatives, as in *I don't know* and *Did you send it?*

In addition the verb *to do* retains the meaning of 'to fare' as originally in the second *do* of the now formalised greeting *How do you do?*

The verb can also be used with an unspecified meaning, as in *She is doing something upstairs*. The meaning may, however, be unspecified because it is conveyed by an accompanying word or by the context in which the remark is being made, as in *He did the washing up* and *Look at me. I can do it now*.

Finally *do* can be used as a substitute pro-verb repeating a verb already mentioned, as in *She likes country music and I do too* ('I like country music').

Task | Look at the following sentences which contain examples of the verb *do* in various forms. How is it being used in each sentence?

    a. *Don't do as I do; do as I tell you.*

    b. *Hullo. I haven't seen you lately. How have you been doing?*

    c. *I don't do the shopping, do you?*

    d. *I repeat: I did see the accused running away.*

    e. *Do as you would be done by.*

    f. *He doesn't smoke, nor does he drink.*

    g. *Don't just stand there. Do something.*

    h. *He does like bananas after all.*

    i. *Where does that leave the situation?*

    j. *I did look at what he was doing.*

Exploration 10 • *Present Participle (1)*

Consider the following sentence:

a. *She watched Anna mowing the lawn.*

It is in fact a combination of

b. *She watched Anna* and

c. *Anna was mowing the lawn.*

Sentences such as:

d. *The man, hearing a noise, rang the police,* and

e. *Miss Smith has a struggle to make ends meet, living as she does on a small pension.*

are combinations of a similar kind. These combinations involve omitting the common element (*Anna, The man, Miss Smith*) and changing a verb into its present participle form (*mowing, hearing, living*).

Task | Look at the following sentences that have this structure. What is the common element that allowed the link to be made? It is possible that there is no common element except by implication, in other words that the participle is unrelated. In that case is the force of the sentence affected?

    a. *Watching the game on television, he fell asleep.*

    b. *He read the name of next Sunday's preacher hanging in the porch.*

    c. *They don't look your own teeth, considering your age.*

    d. *The man examining the tickets became suspicious.*

    e. *He thought about his friends lying on the beach in Spain.*

    f. *I must have looked a mess, judging by the remarks I overheard.*

    g. *Driving out of the bowls club, his car narrowly missed a cyclist.*

    h. *Coming into the village from the west, you will find our house is the first on the right.*

Further Exploration

Collect examples of ambiguous sentences where the ambiguity arises from a verb being used in two different senses. For example:

a. *She is washing.* (reflexive or non-reflexive verb)

b. *They lay in the barn.* (present tense of *lay* or past tense of *lie*)

c. *Does he mix well?* (transitive or intransitive verb)

d. *She goes to church on Sunday.* (present tense conveying regular habit or future event)

e. *We dispense with accuracy.* (verb with preposition, *dispense with*, or without, *dispense*).

Collect examples of verbs that contain a metaphorical comparison with an animal, for example *to dog, to crane one's neck, to rat, to ram, to ape, to swan around*. Is the comparison being made with the human characteristics traditionally given to those animals in fables and folklore, or is it being made with the animal's actual behaviour?

Further Reading

A University Grammar of English, Randolph Quirk and Sidney Greenbaum, Longman, 1973.

A University Grammar of English Workbook, R. A. Close, Longman, 1974.

11 *Word Classes – Adjectives*

Some words are adjectives. What does this mean? Are all adjectives the same? What can we do with adjectives?

Exploration 1 • *Attributive and Predicative*

The function of an adjective is to qualify a noun, to add further to its meaning. It is possible sometimes to tell an adjective from the form of the word, but this is not always the case. Many common adjectives give no clue to their function in their form, for example *old, small, thin, big, bad*, so we have to look at how they are used.

In English an adjective is normally placed before the noun it qualifies as in *a white wall, a magnificent throw*, or it is used as a complement after a copula verb as in *Peaches are delicious* or *My accountant is rich*.

Adjectives used before nouns are called attributive adjectives; adjectives used as verb complements are called predicative adjectives.

Task | Most adjectives in English can be used both attributively and predicatively, as in *The hungry cat* and *The cat is hungry*. However, there are some adjectives that can only be used in the attributive position and some that can only be used predicatively. Look at the following list of adjectives. Which ones can be used in both positions, which can only be found in an attributive position and which only in a predicative position? Are there any uncertain cases?

green, shorter, eventual, enthusiastic, other, friendly, ill, former, strange, liable, sole, main.

Adjectives can sometimes be used directly after a noun, as in *a court martial* and *the president elect*, though this is not normally the case.

Task | Look at the following expressions with an adjective placed after its noun. Which do you find acceptable English expressions and which not?

heir presumptive, the person responsible, the sun hot, the witnesses hostile, the procurator fiscal, all creatures great and small, the mother expectant, the rumour current, the manager designate, the crowd angry.

Exploration 2 • *Intensifying*

Task Some adjectives are used to intensify the meaning of the accompanying noun, as in *sheer folly* and *absolute emergency*. Look at the following list of nouns qualified by intensifying adjectives. State which adjectives can be used, in your opinion:

a. only in the attributive position,

b. both attributively and predicatively without any change of meaning,

c. both attributively and predicatively, but with different meanings depending on their position,

d. both attributively and predicatively with more than one meaning possible in either position.

a. *a complete collapse*   f. *a regular pest*

b. *a mere diversion*   g. *utter madness*

c. *a superb race*   h. *a proper idiot*

d. *a sure winner*   i. *the entire family*

e. *an old friend*   j. *a definite reply*

Exploration 3 • *Limiting*

Task Some adjectives are used to limit or particularise the meaning of the accompanying noun, as *same* in *the same noise*. Look at the following list of adjectives and nouns. Which adjectives are being used as limiters in the manner of 'same' and which ones as intensifiers?

a. *a perfect fool*   f. *a delicious taste*

b. *a massive debt*   g. *the other direction*

c. *a particular reason*   h. *a different picture*

d. *an only son*   i. *an identical chair*

e. *the very man*   j. *a flagrant defiance*

Exploration 4 • *Restrictive*

If you talk about *a white rose*, the adjective *white* gives a more restricted characterisation of *rose*, ruling out *a red rose*, or *a yellow rose*.

Intensifiers heighten the impact of the noun they qualify, limiters narrow down the choice between examples of the same noun, whereas restrictive adjectives define more closely the inherent characteristics of the noun they qualify. In *artificial silk* the adjective *artificial* restricts more closely the qualities we can attribute to the noun, compared with the use of *silk* on its own.

Task Look at the following adjectives and nouns and state whether you consider the adjective is being used:

    a. in a restrictive sense,

    b. in a non-restrictive sense,

    c. with both a restrictive and a non-restrictive interpretation possible, as in *my poor friend*.

a. *a rotten apple*	f. *a hot day*
b. *a silent film*	g. *a dear object*
c. *a rich aunt*	h. *a nice house*
d. *a complete picture*	i. *pure orange juice*
e. *a fresh egg*	j. *plain blackmail*

Exploration 5 • *Stative and Dynamic*

Adjectives are more likely to be stative than dynamic, and in such cases they will not take the progressive aspect of the copula when they are used predicatively. For example, *deep* is unacceptable in the sentence **The water is being deep*. On the other hand a dynamic adjective such as *naughty* accepts use with the progressive aspect of the copula as in *The boy was being naughty*.

Task Look at the following list of adjectives and decide which ones

    a. are stative in use,

    b. are dynamic in use,

    c. could be used in either way.

In the last case do the different uses involve a change of meaning?

careful, high, noisy, thin, brown, bad, lazy, weak, sordid, hard.

Exploration 6 • *Gradable and Non-gradable*

Most adjectives can be used to express a comparison, for example *lighter* or *more suspicious*. They can also be used with other forms of intensification, for example *so nice, very unpleasant, most kind, highest*. There are, however, some adjectives which are not gradable in this way.

Task Look at the following list and state which of the adjectives in it you consider gradable and which non-gradable. If an adjective can be both gradable and non-gradable, does a change of meaning accompany the change of use?

surgical, absolute, manual, Atlantic, unique, mechanical, supreme, tenacious, microscopic, immaculate.

Exploration 7 • *Possessive and Demonstrative*

Adjectives can convey possessive and demonstrative meaning, for example *Hold my case* (possessive) or *Look at those people* (demonstrative).

Pronouns, replacing a noun, can be used in a similar way, for example *That one's mine* (possessive) and *Look at those!* (demonstrative).

Task Which of the following sentences include a demonstrative and which a possessive? Which are adjectives and which are pronouns?

a. *Take this.*
b. *That is annoying.*
c. *Where is that dog?*
d. *Those are the ones.*
e. *I like those cakes.*
f. *These are yours.*
g. *Whose are these shoes?*
h. *Pass my jacket.*
i. *Your decision is yours alone.*
j. *It's not in its box.*

Exploration 8 • *Nouns and Adverbs used as Adjectives*

Some adjectives are related to adverbs, as in *a narrow escape* and *to escape narrowly*. Other adjectives are derived from nouns, as in *a telephonic communication* and *a communication by telephone*. The latter could also be stated as *a telephone communication*, in which *telephone* retains its noun form but is used adjectivally.

Task Look at the following expressions and state whether you consider the adjectives in them:

a. to be derived from an adverb,
b. to be derived from a noun,
c. to be nouns being used as adjectives.

a. *a logical argument*
b. *sexual awareness*
c. *a hard worker*
d. *a town hall*
e. *a quick eater*
f. *a sharp bend*
g. *an alcoholic drink*
h. *a railway worker*
i. *a toll bridge*
j. *a fast food chain*

Exploration 9 • *Adjectival and Pronominal*

Task | Look at the following sentences, each one containing a word underlined. Is the underlined word being used as an adjective or a pronoun?

  a. *No noise, please.*
  b. *Which tie is this?*
  c. *Whose are these?*
  d. *Each time it is the same.*
  e. *None have been lost so far.*
  f. *Many were called.*
  g. *Each deserves a medal.*
  h. *What time is it?*
  i. *Whatever crimes he has committed, he is still my son.*
  j. *Have you many relations?*

Exploration 10 • *Adjectival Expressions*

The function of adjectives can be performed by phrases of more than one word, as in *that never to be forgotten day*, or *the man who played right half for Aston Villa in the late thirties*, where the underlined words form a single unit qualifying the nouns *day* and *man*.

Task | Look at the following expressions. Which words in them make up adjectival expressions?

  a. *the day war broke out*
  b. *the man knocking at the door*
  c. *an any town anywhere design*
  d. *the most domineering person I've ever met*
  e. *deaf and hard of hearing people*
  f. *the woman I met yesterday has called*

Exploration 11 • *Present Participles (2)*

When we considered the present participle in 10 Exploration 10, we were in fact only considering it in its verbal use. It can also be used adjectivally. In *a man charming a snake*, for example, the present participle *charming* is being used verbally, but in *a charming man* it is being used adjectivally.

Task | Look at the following expressions and say whether the verb forms ending in *-ing* are:

a. part of the progressive aspect of a verb,
b. the present participle being used verbally,
c. the present participle being used adjectivally.

a. *She likes cooking apples.*
b. *She hires out rowing boats.*
c. *They are playing cards.*
d. *These are trying times.*
e. *I hate drinking chocolate.*
f. *He's repairing the washing machine.*

Do any of the sentences allow more than one interpretation? If so, can ambiguity be avoided by a change in the stress?

Exploration 12 • *Past Participles*

In 10 Exploration 4 we came across the past participle form of a verb, as in *fetched, wasted* and *seen*. It was used in forming the present perfect tense, as in *I have fetched it, We've wasted our time, They haven't seen me.* Like the present participle it can be used:

a. in forming the tense of a verb,
b. verbally, as *heated* in *He used water already heated on the stove,*
c. adjectivally, as *heated* in *There was a heated exchange of words.*

Task | Look at the following sentences. Are the past participle forms:

a. part of the tense of a verb?
b. used verbally?
c. used adjectivally?

a. *Have we reserved seats?*
b. *Has he had coddled eggs before?*
c. *It is woven material.*
d. *They had toasted muffins for tea.*
e. *We like fresh ground coffee.*
f. *He has developed ideas on the matter.*

Do any of the sentences allow for more than one interpretation? If so, can the ambiguity be avoided by change in the stress?

Further Exploration

Collect for your *Data Book* examples of ambiguous sentences, where the ambiguity arises from different ways of viewing an adjective.

Collect examples of striking similes based on adjectives. Collect examples based both on alliteration, in which the adjective and the word of comparison begin with the same sound, as /b/ in *as bold as brass* and /p/ in *as pleased as punch*, and examples based on the meaning of the word of comparison, as in *as innocent as a new born babe* or *as artful as a waggonload of monkeys*. How often are these two types of simile combined, as in *as dull as ditchwater* or *as proud as a peacock*?

Collect in your *Data Book* examples of oxymoron and transferred epithet that you have identified in everyday, as opposed to a more literary, language usage. Oxymoron is a figure of speech linking together contradictory words to make a special effect out of their apparent conflict of meaning, as in *an open secret, I'll give you a definite maybe* (a Goldwynism – see 8 Exploration 1), *genuine simulated diamonds* (a magazine advertisement). Adjectives are not necessarily involved in this figure of speech, but they usually are. A transferred epithet is an adjective qualifying a noun, but belonging in sense elsewhere in the sentence, as in *We approached a blind corner, I spent many weary hours waiting, The chicken pie was waiting, all eager and tantalising, The tooth is now back in his grateful mouth* (report on an accident in which a boy lost a tooth which was then replaced by a surgeon).

Further Reading

A University Grammar of English, Randolph Quirk and Sidney Greenbaum, Longman, 1973.
A University Grammar of English Workbook, R. A. Close, Longman, 1974.

12 Word Classes – Adverbs

Some words are adverbs. What does this mean? Are all adverbs the same? What can we do with adverbs?

Exploration 1 • Sentence Adverbs

As their name implies, adverbs have the function of qualifying verbs. Adverbs can, however, also be found qualifying adjectives, other adverbs, noun phrases and complete sentences.

Let us look at adverbs qualifying complete sentences. In the sentences *She probably phoned earlier* and *Clearly the man is not to be trusted*, *probably* and *clearly* qualify the whole idea that *She phoned earlier* and *The man is not to be trusted*. They could be replaced with expressions like *It is probable that . . .* and *It is clear that . . . .* The difference between these two sentence adverbs is that *clearly* can also qualify a verb, as in *He can see clearly again after the operation on his eyes*, whereas *probably* cannot.

Task | Look at the following sentences containing adverbs which qualify the whole sentence. State which of these sentence adverbs can also be used, like *clearly*, to qualify individual verbs and which ones, like *probably*, cannot.

    a. *Hopefully he will arrive on time.*
    b. *Luckily it missed the cat.*
    c. *Unfortunately I cannot come tomorrow.*
    d. *You must obviously be exhausted.*
    e. *Regretfully there is not room for your car.*
    f. *I don't agree, actually.*
    g. *Frankly, he's a bore.*
    h. *I will certainly check that.*
    i. *He was possibly unfit.*
    j. *They'll come later presumably.*

Exploration 2 • *Adverbs of Time*

When an adverb qualifies a verb with a reference to time, that reference can be to:

a. time when, as in *She called yesterday,*

b. time how long (duration), as in *He is staying temporarily,* or

c. time how often (frequency), as in *Trains leave hourly.*

Task | Look at the following adverbs of time and state which ones convey time when, which ones convey duration and which ones convey frequency.
weekly, recently, often, annually, now, continuously, finally, periodically, regularly, permanently.

Exploration 3 • *Adverbs of Place*

When an adverb qualifies a verb with a reference to place, the reference can be to:

a. a static position, as in *He lay underneath,* or

b. movement in a certain direction, as in *He stepped forwards.*

Task | Look at the adverbs underlined in the following sentences and state which ones convey an idea of static position and which ones an idea of direction. Could an adverb of static position be used as an adverb of direction in a different context or with a different verb?

a. *He sailed <u>northwards</u>.*
b. *We'll stay <u>here</u>.*
c. *The dog sleeps <u>outside</u>.*
d. *My friends drove <u>home</u>.*
e. *She went <u>abroad</u>.*
f. *She sat <u>inside</u>.*
g. *They went <u>upstairs</u>.*
h. *The car turned <u>left</u>.*
i. *The baby cowered <u>underneath</u>.*
j. *A crowd stood <u>nearby</u>.*

Exploration 4 • *Adverbs of Manner, Method and Instrument*

Adverbs can qualify a verb by presenting an answer to the question 'How?'. Adverbs that define how something is done, can be describing:

a. the manner of the action of the verb, as *quickly* in *She reacted quickly,*

b. the method, as *surgically* in *He was treated surgically,* or

c. the instrument, as *visually* in *He examined it visually.*

Task | Look at the following adverbs and state whether they express manner, method or instrument.

telegraphically, deliberately, obstinately, arithmetically, alphabetically, courageously, nervously, eagerly, slowly, orally.

One way of being able to distinguish between adverbs of manner and adverbs of method or instrument is that adverbs of manner can be qualified by an emphasising adverb, such as *very* as in *She was speaking very slowly*, whereas adverbs of method or instrument cannot (**He was being examined very orally*).

Task | Look at the following adverbs. Each one can be used as an adverb of manner, as *mechanically* in *She was moving very mechanically*, or as an adverb of method (or instrument), as *mechanically* in *The car was sound mechanically*. State the two different senses in which they can be used.

diplomatically, physically, economically, theatrically, theoretically, scientifically, miscroscopically, synthetically, sexually, militarily.

Exploration 5 • *Adverbs of Degree*

The function of an adverb can be to emphasise the meaning of the word or words it qualifies. For example *very* in *She was speaking very slowly* highlights the idea of slowness, *absolutely* in *I absolutely agree* highlights the idea of agreement, *hardly* in *I hardly know him* highlights the level of acquaintance. These highlighting adverbs are sometimes referred to as adverbs of degree. They can either heighten the effect, as in the use of *very* and *absolutely*, or they can make it more muted, as in the case of *hardly*.

Task | Look at the following sentences containing examples of these adverbs and state whether the adverb in each case heightens the effect of the verb it qualifies or makes it more muted.

  a. *His answer was somewhat bewildering.*

  b. *He literally shut his eyes.*

  c. *I really can't tell you.*

  d. *I fully appreciate your reluctance to talk.*

  e. *I barely slept a wink last night.*

  f. *She rather reminds me of Mrs Sweeney.*

  g. *I simply stood there motionless.*

  h. *She quite likes him.*

Exploration 6 • *Adverbial Expressions*

Task | Adverbs can consist of more than one word, as in *at the present time, in the cupboard, little by little, to all intents and purposes.* Look at the following sentences and identify the adverbial expressions they contain, stating what kind they are.

    a. *She was just about on the quay for the boat's arrival.*

    b. *They travelled to the office by bus every morning.*

    c. *Frances grows petunias in her window box.*

    d. *Of course they will go to town on Saturday morning as usual.*

    e. *He cut himself with his razor while shaving.*

    f. *The day before yesterday the wind blew like a hurricane.*

Task | Each of the following sentences contains an adverbial expression introduced by the prepositions *by* or *with*. What kind of adverbial expression is being introduced by the preposition in each sentence?

    a. *We met him by Woolworth's.*   f. *He cleaned it with a sponge.*

    b. *They came by night.*   g. *They repaid the debt with interest.*

    c. *She went by air.*   h. *I'll do it with pleasure.*

    d. *They arrived by chance.*   i. *She did it with a smile.*

    e. *We cook by gas.*   j. *The train will be on time with luck.*

Exploration 7 • *Adverbs with Nouns, Adjectives and other Adverbs*

Adverbs can be used to qualify:

a. nouns, as *rather* in *That is rather an imposition,*

b. adjectives, as *completely* in *They were completely indifferent,*

c. other adverbs, as *very* in *She always knitted very quickly,* and

d. prepositions, as *right* in *They charged right into the crowd.*

Task | Look at the following sentences. What adverbs or adverbial expressions do they contain? Which word class do they qualify?

    a. *She was extremely angry.*

    b. *A police car stood close by the scene.*

    c. *The dog jumped right over the gate.*

    d. *I am so grateful to you.*

    e. *You have made rather a nonsense of that.*

    f. *She replied very brusquely.*

Task | Look at the following adjectives with the nouns they qualify. Each pair could be rewritten as a verb qualified by an adverb, as in *a short visit* changing to *to visit briefly* or *a powerful hit* changing to *to hit hard*. Rewrite each pair as verbs qualified by adverbs.

a. *a sudden alteration*   f. *an oral tradition*

b. *a pure fabrication*   g. *a hasty departure*

c. *an unbearable pain*   h. *a sharp rejoinder*

d. *a thorough job*   i. *an extra place*

e. *an impenetrable barrier*   j. *a comfortable advantage*

Further Exploration

Collect examples of ambiguity arising from different ways of interpreting an adverb. For example:

a. *She is travelling abroad.* (static location or direction)

b. *He was looking on hopefully.* (sentence adverb or manner)

c. *She was quite exhausted.* (heightening or making more mute)

d. *He is permanently staying with us.* (how long or how often)

e. *They turned right smartly.* (direction or qualification of another adverb)

Can these sentences be made unambiguous when spoken, because of the placement of the stress or intonation?

Collect examples of striking similes that are adverbial expressions, as *He speaks to me as if he is addressing a public meeting* or *They behaved as if butter wouldn't melt in their mouths.*

Further Reading

A University Grammar of English, Randolph Quirk and Sidney Greenbaum, Longman, 1973.

A University Grammar of English Workbook, R. A. Close, Longman, 1974.

13 Sentence Structure – Simple Sentences

We move on now to consideration of a larger unit of grammar – the sentence. We see that there is more to a sentence than just a string of words. What are the implications of the different forms of the simple sentence? What does each form tell us about the speaker – and about the relationship between speaker and hearer?

Exploration 1 • Subject and Predicate

In the examination of word structure and word classes we have already begun considering aspects of sentence structure. This was unavoidable since part of the meaning of a word is how it is used in the context of a sentence.

Let us begin the analysis of simple sentence structure by looking at the subject and predicate of a sentence. In the sentences

a. *The Avon lady left a catalogue.*
b. *The man next door sold his garden to a developer.*
c. *The chairs are on the patio.*
d. *Mark wants to be a policeman.*
e. *The car stalled.*

The Avon lady .... *left a catalogue*
The man next door .... *sold his garden to a developer*
The chairs .... *are on the patio*
Mark .... *wants to be a policeman*
The car .... *stalled*

the first half of the sentence is the subject, the second half is the predicate. The subject can be composed of just one word, *Mark*, or a phrase, *The man next door*, but in either case it is the topic on which comment is about to be made in the form of the predicate.

Task | Divide the following sentences into subject and predicate.
a. *She gave the grandfather clock to her niece.*
b. *All the first class seats were full.*
c. *The first sprinter in the 4×100 metres relay team did not pass the baton properly to the next runner.*

d. *The visitor remained silent the whole evening.*
e. *Fortunately the clouds that threatened rain earlier in the day have disappeared.*
f. *She gave me an oil painting of some flowers as a thank-you present.*

Exploration 2 • *Complements and Objects*

The predicate of a sentence will contain a verb, which may be a copula, transitive or intransitive. In the case of a copula the verb is followed by a complement, as in:

a. *Tiddles was hungry.*
b. *Mr Pettigrew became a social worker.*
c. *My mother was a baker in Hull.*

although the copula may be followed by an adverbial expression alone, as in:

d. *My mother was in Hull.*

In the case of a transitive verb a direct object will follow, as *the cherries* in *The boy picked the cherries*, or will be understood, as in *She drank*. Certain verbs will also allow an indirect object which shows who the action of the verb was directed towards, as for example the underlined portion of:

e. *The nurse gave the medicine to the patient.*

which can also be phrased as

f. *The nurse gave the patient the medicine.*

An intransitive verb is not followed by a direct or an indirect object.

Task | Identify the complements, the direct objects and the indirect objects, in the sentences of 14 Exploration 1.

Exploration 3 • *Active and Passive*

Let us consider further the sentence *The nurse gave the patient the medicine*. As it stands *The nurse* is the subject, or the topic of the sentence. However we might wish to make one of the objects into the subject, to place the attention on *the patient* or *the medicine* as the topic on which comment is to be made, as in:

a. *The patient was given the medicine by the nurse.*
b. *The medicine was given to the patient by the nurse.*

To do this we have transformed the simple active sentence structure by means of the passive construction, in which an object becomes the subject and the verb is formed by the appropriate tense of the verb *be* followed by the past participle.

Task Look at the following examples of passive sentences. Was the subject of them a direct or an indirect object in the underlying active sentence?

  a. *The judge was handed a note by the clerk of the court.*
  b. *The traffic was diverted away from the road works.*
  c. *The protestors were persuaded to move by the police.*
  d. *The couple were given a rousing send-off.*
  e. *The flowers were delivered to her dressing room.*
  f. *I have already been seen by the doctor.*

Exploration 4 • *Commands*

When uttering a sentence, the speaker may wish to focus on the verb (and any words depending on it), as in:

a. *Go!*
b. *Look out!*
c. *Catch!*
d. *Mind your own business!*
e. *Don't feed the dog at table!*

The context indicates that the listeners are the ones to whom these commands are directed, but the speaker may wish to emphasise that by saying:

f. *You be quiet!*
g. *Don't you talk to me like that!*
h. *No, you go first!*

Alternatively the speaker may wish to refer to just some of the listeners, as in:

i. *All those with blue tickets go to the right!*
j. *Joel stay behind; the rest go!*

or to people other than them. In the latter case the structure changes to:

k. *Let me make certain first!*
l. *Let us now praise famous people!*

Task Look at the following sentences and state whether they are of the command type outlined here, or whether they are of the subject–predicate type. Are there any which could be either, depending on interpretation?

  a. *Everybody loves a lover.*
  b. *You put the other end down.*
  c. *Someone shut the door.*
  d. *Finish your ice creams, children.*
  e. *You have good weather too.*
  f. *Britons go home.*
  g. *John play for me.*
  h. *Stop me and buy one.*
  i. *You let us enjoy ourselves.*
  j. *Keep out of the reach of babies.*

Exploration 5 • *Apposition*

In sentences such as:

a. *Liverpool, the current holders of the title, were beaten today.*

b. *The boy was reading about Puff, the magic dragon.*

c. *She entrusted her case to a lawyer, an expert in tax matters.*

the words *Liverpool, Puff* and *lawyer* are followed by more information about them. This extra information is placed in apposition to *Liverpool, Puff* and *lawyer*.

Task | Look at the following sentences and identify examples of apposition. Identify any passive or command structure too.

    a. *Mary Queen of Scots was beheaded in 1587.*

    b. *Please send your contributions to the organisers, the Campaign for Famine Relief.*

    c. *Tom, the piper's son, stole a pig.*

    d. *Sredni Vashtar, Lord of Creation, hear my prayer.*

    e. *Susan was born in 1968, a healthy bouncing baby.*

    f. *Don't put your daughter on the stage, Mrs Worthington.*

Exploration 6 • *Syntactic and Semantic Relations*

If we consider the sentences:

a. *Fred opened the door.*

b. *The key opened the door.*

c. *The door opened.*

d. *The winner received a cheque.*

e. *The garage contains the rest of the furniture.*

f. *Tuesday was my birthday.*

we can see that *Fred, The key, The door, The winner, The garage, Tuesday* are all subjects of simple structure sentences. Yet even though the formal or syntactic structure of the sentences may be the same, we understand each of the subjects in a different way: they have a different meaning or semantic relationship with the rest of the sentence.

a. *Fred* is the agent for opening the door.

b. *The key* is the instrument for opening the door.

c. *The door* is the object of the opening.

d. *The winner* is the person to whom the cheque is given.

e. *The garage* indicates the place where the furniture is.

f. *Tuesday* indicates the time of the birthday.

Task | Look at the following sentences, which all have the same syntactic structure, but which have different semantic relations between subject and verb. State in each case whether those relations make the subject feel to be the agent of the verb, the instrument by which it is carried out, the recipient of its action, the object of its action, or its place or time of happening.

   a. *The wall has damp patches.*
   b. *The car stopped.*
   c. *Jane attracted much attention.*
   d. *Monday is closing day for entries.*
   e. *The crane hoisted the load.*
   f. *The glass shattered.*
   g. *The waiter brought the water.*
   h. *The salesman rang the bell.*
   i. *The camera caught the expression on her face.*
   j. *The motorway was congested.*

Exploration 7 • *Linkage and Parataxis*

If two sentences are placed next to each other, they will be understood as linked to one another in sense, even if there is no word making the connection clear. For example,

a. *There was a loud bang. The crowd scattered.* or

b. *The bell rang. The man went to the door. The milk boiled over on the stove.*

We assume that the crowd scattered because of the bang, that the milk was neglected because the man went to the door. This is known as parataxis.

Alternatively the sentences, though separate structures, may contain words like *however, otherwise, on the contrary* whose function is to link with the sense of the previous sentence in a more explicit way, as in:

c. *You may be right. However the facts are against you.*

Task | Look at the following pairs of sentences and say whether they are linked merely as a result of juxtaposition (parataxis) or whether there is a particular word or expression that specifies the linkage.

   a. *The protestors lay down in the road. However the police took no action.*
   b. *Father went out to buy a loaf. There was nobody in the house.*
   c. *The pay is good. On the other hand the conditions of work are poor.*

    d. *I received a tax rebate. As a result we had a holiday in Spain.*

    e. *The clock struck eleven. The lights went out.*

    f. *The chairman banged her gavel. Even so the committee did not pay attention.*

Further Reading

A University Grammar of English. Randolph Quirk and Sidney Greenbaum, Longman, 1973.

A University Grammar of English Workbook, R. A. Close, Longman, 1974.

14 *Sentence Structure – Compound and Complex Sentences*

We now extend our look at sentences to the more complex combinations of simple sentences. Is there any limit to the length of a sentence? Is this a restriction on how we use language? What use do we make of the alternatives open to us?

Exploration 1 • *Coordinating Conjunctions*

If we wish to link two sentences together to make a longer one, we can do so with the word *and*, as in:

a. *John laid the table and Jane carved the meat.*

If we wish to introduce an idea of alternative possibility into the linkage, the word *or* is used, as in:

b. *A siren will sound or bells will be rung.*

If we wish to introduce an idea of reservation or contradiction, the word *but* is used, as in:

c. *The engine left the rails, but the carriages remained on the track.*

If we wish to introduce a causal relationship, the word *for* is used, as in:

d. *John changed hurriedly, for the guests were due at any moment.*

Words like *and*, *or* and *but* are called coordinating conjunctions.

When the sentences linked in this way have words in common or references in common, their second occurrence can be omitted or pronouns or other pro-forms substituted, as in:

e. *John laid the table and (John) poured the wine.*

f. *John tried to unscrew the lid of the mustard pot, but he couldn't manage it.*

Task | Join the following pairs of simple sentences together by means of the coordinating conjunction in brackets. In the resulting, compound, sentence, identify where it is possible to leave words out, and where substitution by pronouns or pro-verbs is possible. Are there any instances where you might reject the use of a pro-form? If so, for what reason?

a. *The waiter brought the food. The waiter served the food to the guests. (and)*

b. *I wanted to buy the pictures. The pictures were too expensive to buy. (but)*

   c. *The cow gave birth to a calf. The calf died half an hour later.* (and)/(but)

   d. *Michael used to go to school by bicycle. His brother used not to go to school by bicycle.* (but)

   e. *The manager wrote to the customer. The customer had gone into the red.* (for)

   f. *The visitors drank mineral water. The visitors had a long way to drive afterwards.* (for)

   g. *The boy could knit. The boy could mend holes in socks. The boy liked embroidery.* (and)

   h. *The masked man pulled out his revolver. The masked man pointed it at the bank clerk. The bank clerk refused to hand over any money to the masked man.* (and)/(but)

A coordinating conjunction can be emphasised by additional words:

a. as *too* in *My wife's mother came and her brother did too*, or

b. as *both* in *He both smokes and drinks*.

Task   Look at the following compound sentences. Use the words in brackets alongside to emphasise the conjunction in them.

   a. *You pay up or you leave.* (either)

   b. *The vicar called and the postman called.* (both)

   c. *Edna looks after the house and has a full-time job.* (as well)

   d. *She made the final but failed to win a medal.* (nevertheless)

   e. *The car not only had a puncture but it ran out of petrol.* (as well)

   f. *He bought a video-recorder but bought a number of tapes as well.* (not only)

Exploration 2 • *Subordinating Conjunctions – Noun Clauses*

Consider the following sentences:

a. *That he had an outstanding talent was obvious from the beginning.*

b. *I decided early on that he had an outstanding talent.*

c. *The point was that he had an outstanding talent.*

d. *She was sure that he had an outstanding talent.*

e. *Your argument that he had an outstanding talent is debatable.*

In each case the sentence . . . *he had an outstanding talent* is subordinated to another sentence and is linked to it by the subordinating conjunction *that*. The wording of the sentence is unchanged; in particular it retains its verb in a finite tense (*had*). Sentences which are part of larger ones but retain their verb in a finite tense will be termed *clauses* from now on. A subordinating conjunction therefore links a subordinate clause to a main clause in a sentence, making it a complex sentence, whereas a coordinating conjunction links two main clauses together, making them a compound sentence.

In the five sentences at the beginning of this Exploration the subordinate clauses fill the roles of

a. the subject of the main clause,
b. the direct object of the main clause,
c. complement,
d. complement to the adjective *sure*,
e. being in apposition to *argument*.

> **Task** | Look at the following sentences and state whether they contain a clause that is acting as a subject, a direct object, a complement, or is in apposition.
>
> a. *I know that my Redeemer liveth.*
> b. *He was happy that no one was hurt.*
> c. *That she answered the telephone at all was a surprise in itself.*
> d. *The player's claim that he had been pushed was rejected.*
> e. *The organiser felt she had been let down.*
>
> To what extent can the conjunction *that* be omitted?

Exploration 3 • *Relative Clauses*

Subordinate clauses can be used to fulfil an adjectival function, in which case they are usually termed relative clauses and are linked to the noun they describe by a relative pronoun, for example *who, which, that, whose.*

> **Task** | Look at the following sentences and state which ones contain relative clauses and which contain noun clauses.
>
> a. *Here is the record that you've all been waiting for.*
> b. *She considers that whist is a tedious game.*
> c. *The lady whose house we rented in Kent is an expert on daffodils.*
> d. *The fact that you were absent is irrelevant.*

In a relative clause the relative pronoun can act as the subject of the clause, as in

a. *The man who came to dinner . . .*

as the direct object of the clause, as in

b. *The actress who(m) everybody wants to see . . .*

as the indirect object of the clause, as in

c. *The policeman who he made the remark to . . .*
   (*The policeman to whom he made the remark . . .*)

as a possessive, as in

d. *The garden whose hedge needed trimming . . .*

as part of an adverbial expression after a preposition, as in

e. *The ease with which he took the lead . . .*

Task Look at the following sentences containing relative clauses. What is the function of the relative pronoun in each case?

What restrictions are there on the contexts in which *who, that, which, whom* and *whose* can be used? Under what circumstances can a relative pronoun be omitted?

a. *the lady who was speaking to me*
b. *the man I was talking to*
c. *a cake that he had baked himself*
d. *the light which I saw in the sky*
e. *the patient whom the nurse was pushing in a chair*
f. *the dog which was barking so loudly*
g. *the woman whose name I always forget*

Exploration 4 • *Adverbial Clauses*

Subordinate clauses can fulfil an adverbial function. They can, for example, be adverbial clauses of time, as in

a. *when I laid the table*

adverbial clauses of place, as in

b. *where the wild thyme grows*

adverbial clauses of condition, as in

c. *if all the world were paper and all the sea were ink*

adverbial clauses of concession, as in

d. *although he's not very tall for a goalkeeper*

adverbial clauses of reason or consequence, as in

e. *because it's there*

adverbial clauses of purpose, as in

f. *so that the neighbours won't see*

adverbial clauses of result, as in

g. *with the result that (so that) the reservoir was empty*

adverbial clauses of comparison, as in

h. *(She is a better writer) than I ever was*

adverbial clauses of manner, as in

i. *in the way that I told you to fold it.*

Task Look at the following sentences. Identify the type of adverbial clause in each case.

a. *As the hart pants for cooling streams, so longs my soul for God.*
b. *They rushed to the exit as soon as the final whistle went.*
c. *Since you're here, you had better come in.*

   d. *Wherever you may roam, there's no place like home.*
   e. *You may go out to play after you've tidied up.*
   f. *Given that the facilities are bad, the results are impressive.*

Exploration 5 • *Non-finite Clauses*

Subordinate clauses can occur in English without a verb in a finite tense. In such non-finite clauses the verb may be turned into a present participle, as in:

a. *Being an orthodox Jew* (As he was an orthodox Jew), *he would not participate on the Saturday.*

it may be turned into a past participle, as in:

b. *Interrupted by a person from Porlock* (After he had been interrupted by a person from Porlock), *Coleridge was unable to recover his train of thought.*

it may be turned into an infinitive, as in:

c. *I would prefer John not to touch it* (that John did not touch it).

or it may be omitted altogether as in:

d. *They admired the man on the flying trapeze* (who was on the flying trapeze).

Task | Each of the subordinate clauses in the following sentences can be changed into a non-finite clause in one of the above ways. State which type of subordinate clause is involved, and whether its verb is changed into a present participle, a past participle or an infinitive, or whether it is verbless through ellipsis.

   a. *The driver denied she was responsible for the collision.*
   b. *They looked away so that they would avoid being embarrassed.*
   c. *He was liable to become violent when he was drunk.*
   d. *Since we hear the trains all day long we have stopped paying any attention to them.*
   e. *I discovered that a window had been broken.*

Task | Each of the following sentences contains a non-finite clause. Identify the clause in each case, state its type and consider whether a clause with a finite verb would be feasible in the same context. If so, are there contexts in which you would use one, but not the other? Why?

   a. *They wanted him to become a doctor.*
   b. *They must have seen us going.*
   c. *A person needs great stamina to succeed at this sport.*
   d. *Rounding up stray sheep is a tiresome business.*
   e. *They live in a house overlooking the sea.*

Exploration 6 • *Nominalisation*

Verbs in finite subordinate clauses can sometimes be transformed into nouns, as, for example:

a. *The fact that he came was significant.*

can be transformed into:

b. *The fact of his coming was significant.* or

c. *They announced that they were seeking a replacement.*

can be expressed as:

d. *They announced their search for a replacement.*

Look at the subordinate clauses in the following sentences and decide whether the verbs in them can be transformed into nouns. If so, what is the effect of nominalisation on the meaning of the sentence? Does it affect how and when you would use the sentence?

Task
a. *She left a lot of things behind because she had left in a hurry.*
b. *We regret that we weren't able to see you earlier.*
c. *The driver asked where the Hotel Bristol was.*
d. *That we have run out of fuel is the result of your incompetence.*
e. *Tom didn't know when the race would begin.*

Exploration 7 • *Adjectival Expressions instead of Clauses*

In 11 Exploration 1 we looked at the attributive use of adjectives. A relative clause can be transformed into an adjectival expression in the attributive position, as for example:

a. *a baby which has just been born*

can be changed into:

b. *a new-born baby*

Task Look at the following expressions and state the combination of noun plus relative clause from which, in your opinion, it has been derived.

a. *a drinking companion*   f. *a couldn't care less attitude*
b. *a floating dock*   g. *a new-found enthusiasm*
c. *a three-fold salary increase*   h. *a man-made fibre*
d. *long-life milk*   i. *vacuum-packed farmhouse cheese*
e. *French fried potatoes*   j. *a masked ball*

How much of the original meaning is left to be assumed in each case, once the relative clause has been changed to an adjectival expression? How does this affect the meaning and use of the expressions?

Exploration 8 • *Nouns instead of Clauses*

Task Look at the following nouns and state the noun plus relative clause which underlies them in each case, in your opinion.

a. *a mother to be* f. *a test drive*

b. *a do-gooder* g. *a near-miss*

c. *an also-ran* h. *a newcomer*

d. *a good-for-nothing* i. *an income*

e. *a whodunnit* j. *a grown-up*

Exploration 9 • *Changes in Structure for Emphasis*

We saw in 7 Exploration 4 that additional prominence can be given by shifting the nuclear stress to a different syllable. Additional prominence can also be given by altering the structure of a sentence, moving a component of the sentence from the position in which we would normally expect it to occur. For example:

a. *Gradually through the mist came the boat.*

instead of:

b. *The boat came gradually through the mist.*

c. *Thrills galore we've had this afternoon.*

instead of:

d. *We've had thrills galore this afternoon.*

Task Look at the following sentences, all of which contain some kind of structural variation for purposes of emphasis. Identify the nature of that variation and state the underlying structure of the sentence.

a. *Waiting in our studio in Newcastle is Fred Pincett.*

b. *Up popped another target.*

c. *There go my promotion prospects.*

d. *Buy it he said he would and bought it he has indeed.*

e. *Sad it is that he cannot be with us today.*

f. *Playing the piano is something I detest.*

How do these variations affect the meaning or emphasis of the sentence? Are any other grammatical devices, apart from alteration of structure, used for purposes of emphasis. Where would you expect the nuclear stress to be placed in each of these cases?

A further structure that gives added prominence to a component of the sentence is that in which a sentence like:

a. *The hydrangea is withering.*

is changed to:

b. *It is the hydrangea that is withering.* or

c. *He first met her in Whitley Wood.*

is changed to:

d. *It was in Whitley Wood that he first met her.*

Task | Change the following sentences into this structure, thereby giving added prominence to the underlined words.

   a. *The dog died.*
   b. *The man looked at the house next door.*
   c. *Aunt Eva is due tomorrow.*
   d. *I am keeping an eye on you because I don't trust you.*

What is the effect of these changes on the meaning of the sentences?

Further Exploration

Collect examples of ambiguity that occur because two different structures can be given to a sentence, such as:

a. *She promised to send it on Friday.*
b. *I wasn't looking at the time.*
c. *The reporter watched the school play.*
d. *We had our luggage taken.*

Collect examples of anomalous sentences, such as:

a. *He is Europe's other greatest jockey.*
b. *Progress, although slow and steady, was increasing.*

Make a note in your *Data Book* of any rhetorical devices that you find striking. Would you still find them striking if they were more familiar to you? For example:

a. *A gentleman's agreement is not worth the paper it's printed on.* (Another Goldwynism – see 8 Exploration 1.)

This is an example of paradox: an apparent contradiction that on reflection makes sense.

b. *Superficially he's very profound, but deep down he's very superficial.*

This is an example of antithesis, where the arrangement of the words complements the paradoxical thought.

c. *Calcutta is built on silt, London on gravel, Singapore on swamp, Hollywood on dreams.*

This is an example of zeugma, where nouns are related to verbs or adjectives in different ways. Zeugma is in turn a particular form of syllepsis, where sentence components agree in sense but the structure is not satisfactory (*Neither you nor I are in a position to decide*).

Further Reading

A University Grammar of English, Randolph Quirk and Sidney Greenbaum, Longman, 1973.

A University Grammar of English Workbook, R. A. Close, Longman, 1974.

15 *Discourse Structure*

We conclude our look at the sentence by examining other ways we can join them together into longer passages. Once again the question is not simply 'What can we do?', but rather 'What do we do with these forms?' What implications are there in the choice of one form rather than another?

Exploration 1 • *Link Words between Sentences*

We saw in 13 Exploration 7 that sentences could be linked by words and expressions, such as *however, furthermore, as a result*, and *on the other hand*, which direct the attention beyond the limits of the sentence's structure.

Task | Look at the following sentences. Identify the word or expression of linkage that each one contains and state what, in your opinion, its precise function is in the sentence. Does it, for example, introduce a concession (*still, at any rate*), a consequence (*therefore*), an antithesis (*instead, on the contrary*)? Does it sum up (*in short*) or reinforce (*moreover*)?

   a. *Firstly the weather is bad.*

   b. *Anyway I'll see you tomorrow.*

   c. *Finally let us consider Southend.*

   d. *Furthermore I don't like her.*

   e. *Rather he strikes me as a bully.*

   f. *Next he refused to fix the sink.*

   g. *So we came here instead.*

   h. *On the contrary I liked it there.*

   i. *By the way the letter came this morning.*

   j. *Then there's the car to tax.*

Exploration 2 • *Pro-forms*

We saw in 14 Exploration 1 that when sentences are linked structurally, pro-forms can be substituted on the second occurrence of a word or reference. Such substitution also takes place across sentence boundaries. The substitutes can do duty as nouns:

a. as *them* in *The customs officer confiscated them.*

as verbs:

b. as *do* in *I hope to do it soon.*

as adjectives or adjectival expressions:

c. as *his* in *May I present you to his wife?*

as adverbs or adverbial expressions:

d. as *then* and *there* in *Be at the station at eight sharp. I look forward to seeing you there then.*

A pro-form may be used to substitute for a predicate:

e. as *does* in *I like cream. Henry does too.*

or for a whole clause:

f. as *that* in *We are leaving for Marmaris on Wednesday. However you already know that.*

In addition to substitution with pro-forms, repetition can be avoided by omission or ellipsis.

Task | Look at the following pairs of sentences. Identify any pro-forms in the second sentence, state their word class (noun, verb, adjective or adverb) and what word or words they replace. Identify also instances of ellipsis.

a. *Is the manager available to see Mrs Walker tomorrow? His secretary doesn't think so.*

b. *The concrete paving slabs have not yet arrived. However they are expected any day now.*

c. *Insert the needle into the back of the garment and twist the wool round it to make a new stitch. Do this four times.*

d. *Anna finally telephoned her relatives in Hunstanton last night. Of course they asked her why she hadn't done so before then.*

e. *The meeting passed a motion of no-confidence in the president and secretary. These two immediately tendered their resignation, but the treasurer refused to offer hers when asked to do so.*

f. *The singer kept a scrapbook of press cuttings. She not only put her own reviews in it but those of her friends as well.*

Exploration 3 • *Anaphoric and Cataphoric Reference*

Pro-forms can not only direct the attention backwards to words that have already occurred; they can also direct the attention forwards to something not yet mentioned. Whereas *it* in:

a. *Learn to wind-surf; it's easy.*

looks back to *learn to wind-surf* (anaphoric), *it* in:

b. *It is easy to learn to wind-surf.*

looks forward (cataphoric).

Task | Look at the following sentences and decide whether the pro-forms are anaphoric or cataphoric in reference.
a. *You're not going to believe this. I'm getting married.*
b. *If she insists on doing so, for goodness sake let Jane ride her motorcycle to work.*
c. *The crowd surged forward to see but the line of police held their pressure.*
d. *When they build their nests high up in the trees, the saying goes that crows are heralding fine weather.*

Exploration 4 • *Repetition of Reference*

Linkage may be made by referring to a noun by means of another noun, as in:

a. *Pass me the garlic crusher, the thing next to the kettle.*

The reference may be to a part of the original, either specific, as in

b. *The Tippings all came, but only Karen stayed for any length of time.*

or less specific, as in

c. *The tourists wandered through the castle, many of them completely uninterested in what they saw, or*

d. *Stewart upset a glass of port and some of it went onto his trousers.*

Task | Look at the following sentences and state what is the nature of the linking reference in each case.
a. *The thieves clambered into the back seat of a waiting Citroën. The car immediately sped off towards the Latin Quarter.*
b. *The Germans and the Hungarians protested, threatening to boycott the proceedings. In the event only the latter carried out their threat.*

c. *There was a wide selection of flowers on show. The sweet peas were the most impressive.*

d. *All former prime ministers had been invited. Mr Macmillan however was unable to attend.*

Exploration 5 • *Links within a Paragraph*

Task | Look at the following passage. Identify the various devices that the writers have used to link the clauses within each sentence, as well as the devices that link the sentences within the paragraph. State the nature of the devices that you identify.

One of them – the antique-dealer – volunteered. He owned weapons, including a .22 rifle with telescopic sights, and he had the opportunity to install himself in an apartment facing the official building.

So, keeping back a little in order not to be seen, there he was, crouched in the semi-darkness, behind the cheering crowd. He was under no illusions about the gravity of what he was about to do; he knew that by a simple movement of his finger he could change the course of events. But he also knew that he had to do it. For de Gaulle would beat about the bush; he had not changed. Undoubtedly he would give forth some fine phrases but none of them would amount to a formal commitment. The man of Brazzaville would not be able to say that Algeria would remain French, that he had understood local feeling. Otherwise he would be undertaking a commitment which he would be bound to keep. Thirteen years of retirement had certainly not changed him. The best thing for Algeria was to do away with him.

Target: de Gaulle, Christian Plume and Pierre Démaret, Secker & Warburg, 1974 (page 6).

Are there any examples in this excerpt of reference being made to the text before or after it, or of references being made to the situation in which this passage is set? Identify any such examples.

Further Exploration

Analyse other pieces of prose to identify the linking components in them.

Further Reading

A University Grammar of English, Randolph Quirk and Sidney Greenbaum, Longman, 1973.

A University Grammar of English Workbook, R. A. Close, Longman, 1974.

---

16 *Lexical Meaning*

Here we look at aspects of word meaning. How can one word mean several different things? How is it that people can misunderstand the meaning of a word? How many layers of meaning can you find in a word? Where do new words come from?

Exploration 1 • *'Name', 'Thing' and 'Sense'*

If we think in terms of a 'name' as the spoken sound or written shape of a word, then the name is connected in our minds to the 'thing' or non-linguistic phenomenon it refers to, by the 'sense' or information which is conveyed. The reference can be to a specific 'thing', as in 'Mark' or 'Birmingham'; it can be non-specific, as in 'a flower' or 'a handkerchief'.

Task | Look at the following list of words and decide which of them are likely to be used for specific reference as they stand, and which are not:

friend, geranium, Frenchman, Simon, sword, Bootle, boycott, smith, coffee, wellington.

Exploration 2 • *Imaginary Sense*

The name can have a sense that refers to something imaginary, such as *leprechaun,* or to something that is completely abstract, such as *theory.*

Task | Look at the following words and state which ones refer to things in the world of physical existence and which things are creations of the mind:

dwarf, (power of) reason, unicorn, voice, griffon, atmosphere, surprise, theorem, wyvern, soul.

Are there any words about which you cannot decide? If so, why?

Exploration 3 • *Onomatopoeia – Sense and Sound Linked*

The sound of the name can be an imitation of the sound of the thing, as in *cuckoo*. This is onomatopoeia of a clear-cut kind. Less precisely the sound of the name can also be used to evoke a movement, as in *slither*, or a physical or moral quality, as in *nip and tuck* and *mingy*.

Task | Look at the following list and decide which of the words in it are onomatopoeic echoes of the sound and which are made up of sounds that try to evoke a movement or quality. Do any of the words in the list not belong under either definition in your opinion?

swoop, backlash, hum, buzz, tick-tock, wry, ding-dong, niggle, ooze, phew.

Amongst those that you have decided are onomatopoeic, which ones are purely echoes of sounds, either human such as the hesitating *errrr* or non-human such as *ter wit ter woo* of an owl?

Exploration 4 • *Sense Confused by Sound*

If the sound of the name is confused with that of a similar-sounding word, but one with a different sense, the result is often a malapropism.

Task | Identify such confusions of sound in the following contexts. State what you consider the intended sense to be and whether it is a malapropism in your view, i.e. does it provoke humour?

a. *Switzerland introduced female sufferance in 1971.*

b. *The walls were streaming with condescension.*

c. *That mitigated against his acceptance of the idea.*

d. *Immigrants tend to conjugate together in the centre of large towns.*

e. *I will discharge it to the best of my responsibility.*

Exploration 5 • *Senses Confused*

The similarity of sound between two words of different sense is often deliberately exploited. In addition there can be confusion in usage between words of similar senses, leading sometimes to changes in sense.

Task | Look at the following sentences and identify examples of both of these.

    a. *Massage tones up the subterranean tissues.*

    b. *A Zanussi refrigerator – the appliance of science.*

    c. *What are you inferring by your remark?*

    d. *I've been lying on the trick-cyclist's couch all afternoon.*

    e. *I refute your claim absolutely.*

Exploration 6 • *Synonyms – Different Names Same Sense*

In 8 Further Explorations and 9 Exploration 1 we have already considered two particular examples of synonymy (rhyming slang and antonomasia), where two different names possess the same sense.

Task | Look at the names in the first list below and link each one with the name in the second list that seems to you to have the same sense. Consider whether there is in fact any difference in meaning between the pairs you have so linked, bearing in mind Dr Johnson's remark that words are seldom exactly synonymous.

    a. *purchase, sodium chloride, almost, begin, gas, bloody, purvey, sputnik, spud, wireless;*

    b. *petrol, salt, radio, buy, nearly, potato, supply, commence, sanguinary, satellite.*

Exploration 7 • *Homonyms – Same Name Different Senses*

In 6 Exploration 1 we looked at homonyms, both homophonic and homographic.

Task | Look at the following list of words that have at least two distinct, apparently unconnected senses. Give two meanings in each case and use an etymological dictionary to find out whether there is any connection between the two in their derivation.

tree, file, plant, pupil, sole, bull, lawn, pink, stock, tank.

Exploration 8 • *Polysemy – Same Name Varied Senses*

A name can have a number of senses which, though distinct, are linked, for example *right* can mean 'just' or 'correct'. Which meaning is understood depends on the context in which it is being used.

Task | Look at the words below. Each one is followed by the names of people in five different spheres of activity. State what you think would be a sense likely to be given to the name by each person when using it in the course of their activity.

a. *action*   a soldier, a film director, a lawyer, a politician, a cricket coach,

b. *paper*   a newsagent, a stationer, a lecturer, an examinee, a voter.

Are any of the uses distinguished by the structural context, as distinct from the semantic context? For example, teachers talking about corporal punishment would use *beat* as a verb, whereas a policeman walking the *beat* would use it as a noun.

Exploration 9 • *Figurative Extensions of Sense*

One reason for the existence of a variety of senses for the same name lies in the figurative, above all metaphorical, use of words. For example,

a. *to drop something* is literally 'to let something fall', but the verb is used in a metaphorical extension of the sense in *to drop the subject, to drop a hint*.

b. *to grasp* is literally 'to hold firmly', but the verb is used metaphorically in *to grasp the initiative, to grasp the meaning*.

Task | Look at the following sentences. State in each whether the verb used is meant to be understood in a literal sense or a figurative one.

a. *Mother broke the silence at last.*

b. *They cracked codes at Bletchley Park.*

c. *He had dropped his hands.*

d. *The paper aroused my curiosity.*

e. *The police wrestled with the strikers.*

f. *Lavoisier exploded the concept of phlogiston.*

Task | The following sentences allow at least two interpretations, depending on whether there is a literal or a figurative sense understood. State both kinds of interpretation in each case. Identify and explain the word or words at the root of the ambiguity.

a. *He smashed the record.*

b. *She was struck by the flowers.*

c. *It made an impression on me.*

d. *The star was sparkling that evening.*

117

Exploration 10 • *One Sense Included in Another*

If we consider the words *owl, warbler, bird, eagle, tit, nightingale*, we see that *bird* can apply to all the others in the list as they are particular species of bird.

Task | Look at the following lists and state whether there is a name whose sense includes all these:

a. *elm, ash, sycamore, walnut, pine, deal, laurel, teak,*
b. *glass, schooner, mug, tumbler, goblet, beaker,*
c. *car, van, bus, lorry, motorcycle, go-kart, tricycle,*
d. *drizzle, snow, Scotch mist, hail, sleet, rain,*
e. *cocoa, coffee, tea, lemonade, squash, wine, beer,*
f. *brick, sand, cement, mortar, tile, gravel, concrete, wood.*

Exploration 11 • *One Sense Excludes Another*

Whereas Exploration 10 dealt with the idea of inclusion and compatibility of senses, the pairs of words below illustrate exclusion of sense of various kinds.

a. They can be a binary pair which is completely incompatible, as *married* makes it impossible to be *single*.
b. They can be incompatible members of a larger class, as a piece of furniture cannot be a *chair* if it is a *table*.
c. They can be incompatible, as in *old* and *young*, yet variable, since what constitutes 'old' in comparison to 'young' depends on each context. For example, a person of forty will be 'old' for a career in sport but 'young' for appointment as a judge.
d. The pair can be the converse of each other, as *give* is the converse of *take*.

Task | To which of the four categories outlined above do each of these pairs of words belong?

a. *rich/poor*   f. *alive/dead*
b. *in/out*   g. *hat/coat*
c. *borrow/lend*   h. *buy/sell*
d. *male/female*   i. *above/underneath*
e. *please/like*   j. *slow/fast*

Exploration 12 • *Vagueness of Sense*

The sense of a name may lack precision.

a. The sense may be vague, as in *hill*, because, although we have a clear reference to the 'thing' in general, it may be unclear in particular cases. Does *mound* or *tump* belong to the sense of *hill*? Why are the Black Mountains on the South Wales border so called, when their highest point (2660ft) is about the same height as the highest point in the Cheviot Hills (2676ft)?

b. The sense may be vague because it is not possible to determine, since it varies so much according to context. The word *good* varies in sense in *good morning, good hiding, good character, a good look, good work*, not to mention possible variations within those usages. Yet we feel at the same time that the word is homogeneous and not an example of polysemy.

c. We do not know the relationship of *Alec* to *car* when we hear *Alec's car* mentioned out of context. Is it his own, has he borrowed it, is he just driving it for the day and so on?

d. The sense of a name may be vague in that it lacks specifying details. If the police are looking for the *driver* of a car, they may not be able to specify whether the 'driver' is old or young, male or female.

e. The sense of a name may be vague because it covers alternative possibilities, as in an advertisement for a secretary who is either *competent in French and German* or *possesses good shorthand*.

Task | Identify examples of vagueness of sense in the following sentences and state which of the five categories outlined above you think they belong to.

a. *I have new neighbours.*
b. *These are Meg's stamps.*
c. *She has gone to London.*
d. *We are looking for witnesses.*
e. *That's the boss's chair.*
f. *Will the person who did that come forward?*
g. *The person who did that must be naïve or a villain.*
h. *They live in the country.*

Exploration 13 • *Tautology – Repetition of Sense*

If there is a repetition of the sense through the use of different names, the resulting effect is termed tautology.

Task Identify the examples of tautology in the following sentences and state what purpose, if any, the repetition serves, in your opinion.

   a. *He has a great future ahead of him.*

   b. *He is not an orphan, what's more he never was one.*

   c. *The table has a hole pre-cut for a parasol.*

   d. *This is my last will and testament.*

   e. *She ran the race of her life.*

   f. *He was allowed to proceed without let or hindrance.*

   g. *I totally agree with all you say.*

   h. *We intend to get at the true facts of the case.*

Exploration 14 • *Euphemism – Avoiding Specific Names*

A name may be affected by a taboo and be replaced by a new name to convey the same sense. In that case a euphemism has been created.

a. The taboo may come about through fear. Terms like *Old Nick* developed as euphemisms for 'the devil' and 'Satan' in order to avoid saying the names themselves, thereby upsetting the evil one.

b. The taboo may come through a sense of propriety, particularly when sexual relationships, certain bodily parts and functions and swearing are concerned. The terms *lavatory* and *toilet*, originally to do with washing and dressing, have acquired their current senses in this way and in turn are being replaced by *loo* by some English speakers.

c. The taboo may be the result of a sense of delicacy, to avoid embarrassment. The term *disease* began as a euphemism ('lack of ease') for illness; *dying* is often replaced by *passing away*, for example, for the same reason.

Task Identify expressions that you consider to be euphemisms in the following sentences and give the name that you think the speakers or writers wished to avoid using.

   a. *The convicted man has been detained in a correctional facility.*

   b. *The military have contingency plans for the demographic targetting of certain places in Europe.*

   c. *He is a pre-owned vehicle re-allocation specialist.*

Task   d. *They were holding large numbers of administrative detainees in camps near the border.*

e. *The Chancellor of the Exchequer is proposing new revenue enhancement measures.*

f. *This door gives access to exterior space.*

g. *They decided to launch a preemptive strike in the event of an all-out strategic exchange.*

h. *She is expecting.*

i. *I was shocked to hear you use a four letter word.*

j. *He is the purveyor of meat to the Royal Family.*

Exploration 15 • *Anomaly – Conflicting Senses*

Anomaly may arise from the way a sentence is constructed. It also occurs when a sentence contains names with contradictory senses.

Task   Identify examples of the latter kind of anomaly in the following sentences. Consider in each case whether there was some reason for the anomaly occurring.

a. *There was a sticker in the back of the car saying 'Fenland Mountain Rescue'.*

b. *I'll bet you a fiver I'm not a gambling man.*

c. *You're the twentieth person I've told this morning – we have no call for it.*

d. *I want you to make a bust of my wife's hands.* (A Goldwynism: see 8 Exploration 1)

e. *The urge to destroy is a creative urge.*

Exploration 16 • *Sense and Nonsense Words*

Peter Strevens in his *Papers in Language and Language Teaching* (Oxford University Press, 1965, page 77) quotes the following announcement from an issue of the monthly journal *The Motor Boat*:

Grablins coffled to special order.

The announcement was a leg-pull, since there exist no such words in English as *grablin* and *coffle* (as a verb). Yet they could have been taken as existing words of English because they sound like and are used as an English noun and verb.

Task Look at the following sentences. Some contain:

a. non-existent words like *grablin*;

some contain:

b. words which might appear to be inventions, like *gobbledygook*, but which have a settled sense;

and some contain:

c. substitute forms, like *a what-d'you-call-it*, that are in current use to convey a sense that varies according to context.

State which words in the sentences come under each of the three categories outlined above, in your present opinion. Then check in the dictionary.

a. *She is really gimp.*

b. *He is a mugwump.*

c. *Pass the doofer.*

d. *She had read the blurb.*

e. *What's all this guff?*

f. *He's not as biffo as he looks.*

g. *Thingummy can't come.*

h. *It's a wimwom for a mustard mill.*

i. *That's awfully thing of you.*

j. *That is balderdash.*

Further Exploration

Make a note in your *Data Book* of any unusual and striking examples of the points introduced in this chapter, e.g. euphemism, anomaly, malapropism.

Further Reading

Semantics, an Introduction to the Science of Meaning, Stephen Ullmann, Blackwell, 1962.

17 *Structure, Context and Meaning*

Just as meaning is conveyed by our choice of words, it is also conveyed by how we put them together in sentences. How is the meaning of a word affected by how we use it in a sentence? Can different sentences mean quite the same thing? Is there such a thing as the literal meaning of a sentence? What implications, assumptions, and hidden meanings are there in a sentence?

Exploration 1 • *Sense Affected by Structure*

The rearrangement of a sentence may change its sense, as in:

a. *They have to say something/They have something to say,*

or it may change it stylistically, as in:

b. *She advanced slowly/Slowly she advanced.*

Task | Look at the following pairs of sentences. Compare the choice and order of the words in the second sentence with that of the first and say whether the difference between the two changes the meaning or just the way it is presented. Is a new sense given to the words or is the same sense projected in a different way?

    a. *They decided last Sunday to leave.*
      They decided to leave last Sunday.

    b. *The car ran over the dog.*
      The car ran the dog over.

    c. *The woman went off wearing long white gloves.*
      The woman wearing long white gloves went off.

    d. *She still told me that she loved me.*
      She told me that she still loved me.

    e. *Only thirty people will be going.*
      Thirty people will only be going.

    f. *Joining the motorway at the next junction the motorist saw a police car.*
      The motorist saw a police car joining the motorway at the next junction.

Exploration 2 • *Circumlocution*

If the expression of the sense is felt to be circuitous, not as direct as it could be, the term for this is circumlocution or periphrasis.

Task | Look at the following sentences. Consider an alternative way of expressing their sense and whether that way would be more succinct. If there is a more succinct way, is it preferable or would an important stylistic element be lost?

    a. *There are contingency plans to fire a nuclear weapon for demonstrative purposes, to demonstrate to the other side that they are exceeding the limits of toleration in their conventional attack.*

    b. *I have it in command from The Queen to inform your Lordship that Her Majesty has been graciously pleased to appoint you to deliver the Glove to Her Majesty during the Ceremony in Westminster Abbey on the occasion of the Solemnity of Her Majesty's Coronation on the 2nd June next.*

    c. *He résuméed his ideas in a concise summarisation.*

Exploration 3 • *Paraphrase*

Task | Look at the following sentences. They contain expressions that are frequently used in a figurative sense, though they could equally well be used literally. Give a paraphrase of the figurative sense in each case and state whether the listener will know which sense to understand as a result of clues within the sentence, or whether it will be just the wider context of the discourse that indicates the sense.

    a. *I have a number of irons in the fire.*

    b. *She is sitting on the fence.*

    c. *Keep that under your hat.*

    d. *She tested the temperature of the bathwater.*

    e. *The situation is a different ballgame now.*

    f. *They have maintained a low profile in all this.*

    g. *Just keep hanging in there.*

    h. *They blew the whistle on the authorities.*

Exploration 4 • *Deictic Devices – the Physical Context*

In 13 Exploration 7 and 15 Explorations 1 to 5 we considered devices that make links between sentences. These devices place the sense of the sentence in the wider context of the discourse – of what is being said or written.

Language also contains devices that place the sense of a sentence in the context of the physical world. These pointing, or deictic, devices refer to the time and place in which the sentence is being delivered. For example,

a. The pronouns *I, we* and *you* identify the speaker and the person spoken to. When *you* and *I, our* relationship established, are talking about other people and things, we will use pro-forms.

b. If a man on a boat, throwing a rope to someone on the bank, merely shouts *Hold this*, *this* in the particular context directs the attention to the rope without the name *rope* being mentioned at all.

c. In a statement such as *It is raining here now, now* refers to the moment of speaking and *here* to the place, both of them drawing their sense from when and where the statement is made.

Task | Look at the following sentences. Identify the deictic devices they contain. An outline of the non-linguistic context is contained within brackets after each one.

    a. *I think that car is heading straight for us.* (said Gary pointing to a vehicle in the distance)

    b. *This will do.* (said Mary using the back of a spoon to open the treacle tin)

    c. *I'll have the same.* (said the guest at dinner holding out her plate in turn)

    d. *Give me your other one.* (said the doctor examining a casualty's hands)

    e. *Can I help you?* (the shop assistant asked the customer)

    f. *Henry should have been here by now.* (said the anxious mother)

    g. *Well, that's that!* (said the gardener with relief on completing the digging of a large plot)

    h. *In case of fire break the glass.* (notice over a glass-fronted box)

Exploration 5 • *Irony*

If a statement is designed to be understood in a way which is opposed to the sense of the words, then irony is being used. For example, if someone says *John's having a rough time out in Spain* and it is known that John is sitting in the sun sipping champagne, the statement is ironic. The irony might be on a friendly teasing level or it might be on a more serious and therefore sarcastic level.

Task | Imagine the following statements to be ironic. State a possible context in which they would therefore be uttered.

a. *I feel sorry for him in that hotel.*

b. *Don't rush to help, everybody.*

c. *She'll love you for that.*

d. *I cried all the way to the bank.*

How would you know whether these sentences were meant to be ironic or not? Consider the extent to which intonation and stress play a part in conveying each irony.

Exploration 6 • *Hyperbole and Litotes*

If the sense is deliberately exaggerated, as in

a. *The world and his wife telephoned while you were out,*

it is termed hyperbole.

If the sense is deliberately underplayed, as in

b. *The Boston strangler did not help the image of the door-to-door salesman with his activities,*

it is termed litotes or meiosis.

Task | Look at the following sentences, which you should assume are all examples of hyperbole or litotes. State which rhetorical device is involved, in your opinion, in each case and consider whether the effect of the over- or understatement arises from the linguistic context within the sentence or whether a wider context is needed before that can be decided.

a. *This is hardly the moment to complain.*

b. *That was no mean achievement.*

c. *We've had thousands of letters and millions of telephone calls.*

d. *Would you mind terribly if I closed the window a little?*

e. *The matter is just a little local difficulty.*

f. *He was far from being pleased.*

Exploration 7 • *Logical Entailment and Expectation*

In 16 Exploration 11 we looked at pairs of words which had conflicting senses of various kinds. In 16 Exploration 15 we looked at sentences containing contradictions that existed between words in them. Now let us consider contradictions existing between sentences.

If we are told

a. *The postman came this morning*

we would infer that he came to deliver some mail. If we then hear

b. *There was no post today*

we would be faced with a contradiction, but one which could be resolved with an explanation such as,

c. *He came to ask me something*

since we only inferred a mail delivery from the first sentence. Mail delivery is not the only possible reason for the postman coming; it is just the most likely one in the context.

On the other hand, if we are told

d. *The postman brought us two letters this morning*

and then hear

e. *There was no post this* (same) *morning,*

the two sentences are not reconcileable since bringing letters entails there being post.

Task | Look at the following pairs of sentences. State whether the contradiction between the two is merely apparent, being based only on inference and expectation, or whether it is real because the first sentence entails the second.

    a. *Smith's Garages can promise delivery of a new Jaguar in six weeks. (Smith's Garages will receive no new cars for the next two months.)*

    b. *All unimpaired humans learn language.*
    (Hence language is not a sophisticated cognitive ability.)

    c. *The demonstration occurred spontaneously.*
    (Someone was organising the demonstration.)

    d. *The election has not changed anything.*
    (The election was pointless and a failure.)

    e. *Inspector Mitchell has been shot.*
    (Inspector Mitchell will be on duty on Monday.)

    f. *The deductions are based on a false premise.*
    (The deductions are themselves false.)

Exploration 8 • *Presupposition*

There is a traditional question *Have you stopped beating your wife yet?* that is used to illustrate the notion of presupposition. In the way the question is framed it is presupposed that the man addressed not only has a wife; he beats her as well.

What is presupposed in a sentence is that which is taken as accepted, taken for granted. It is the basis for the comment, enquiry, etc. that is being made.

Task | Look at the following sentences and identify what information is taken as agreed in each of them.

   a. *The storm cut off the electricity to our house.*
   b. *The laboratory needs painting again badly.*
   c. *The warder was bribed to help the prisoner escape.*
   d. *Their divorce was not reported in the press.*
   e. *She found a gold coin while diving off the coast of Spain.*
   f. *She played the violin sonata by sight reading.*

Exploration 9 • *True or False Statements*

The validity of a statement can depend on when and where it is made and by whom. It may be true or false because of the way it describes the universe we live in, as in:

a. *Water finds its own level,* and

b. *The moon is made of green cheese.*

but it may also be true or false because of the way it relates to circumstances at the time of its utterance. If the author at the moment of writing this Exploration says

c. *Estonia is an independent country,*

d. *I am moving house next week,* or

e. *My father is hale and hearty,*

these statements are false. Whereas the statements

f. *Estonia used to be an independent country,*

g. *I am moving house next year,* and

h. *My father is no longer alive,*

are true statements in the circumstances.

Task | Look at the following statements and imagine they have been made by you at the time of reading. Decide which statements are true and which false in your circumstances. Are they true or false because of the nature of the universe you live in (*Water finds its own level*), because of the times you live in (*Estonia is an independent country*) or because of your own private circumstances (*My father is hale and hearty*)?

a. *I have two sisters.*

b. *Our house has no gas.*

c. *Our Prime Minister is a woman.*

d. *Deadly nightshade is poisonous.*

e. *Pigs have wings.*

f. *Cyprus is an island.*

A statement may be presented as fact, as in:

a. *She turned the radio on,*

or it may be seen as an assertion, as in:

b. *They should be here.*

When such statements are made subordinate clauses, as in:

c. *I could have sworn that she turned the radio on,* or

d. *It is wrong that they should be here,*

their meaning can be changed.

Task | Look at the following sentences. Decide firstly whether you consider them to be statements of fact (true or false as the case may be) or assertions. Then turn them into subordinate clauses by placing them after the words in brackets alongside. Has the meaning of the original sentence been changed by subordinating it in this way? If so, how has it changed? If you had originally considered it to be a true (false) statement of fact, has it been made any less (more) plausible? Has assertion been turned into fact or vice versa?

a. *Jogging is bad for you.* (Emily thinks that . . .)

b. *Cars are expensive to run.* (Pauline is convinced that . . .)

c. *Paper can be made from rags.* (The Chinese discovered that . . .)

d. *The world is flat.* (George says that . . .)

e. *Men will land on Mars.* (It is nonsense to say that . . .)

f. *He is going to work harder.* (He pretends that . . .)

Exploration 10 • *Sentences as Formulae*

When English children repeat:

a. *She sells seashells beside the sea shore*

or French children repeat:

b. *Les chemises de l'archiduchesse sont sèches*

the point of the repetition is to see whether the sentences can be said without confusion of pronunciation, not for the sense of their words.

Task | Look at the following, which are understood in English for reasons other than the sense of the words they contain. State in each case what context they call to the mind of an English speaker.

a. *The quick brown fox jumped over the lazy dog.*

b. *Peter Piper picked a peck of pickled pepper.*

c. *La plume de ma tante est dans le jardin.*

d. *Eeny meeny miny mo.*

Task | The following sentences have become established as set formulae in English, when used in a particular context. State the context involved, in each case. Can any part of the sentences be changed and they still remain valid in that context?

a. *I name this ship Teresa. May God bless her and all who sail in her.*

b. *On your marks; get set; go!*

c. *I hereby warn you that anything you say may be taken down and used in evidence against you.*

d. *I pronounce you man and wife.*

e. *I swear that the evidence I shall give is the truth, the whole truth and nothing but the truth.*

f. *I name the Member for Harlow.*

g. *I have great pleasure in declaring this bazaar open.*

h. *I promise to pay the bearer on demand the sum of . . .*

How binding are the sentences once uttered? Would any of the functions be regarded as equally valid, if other words were uttered to convey the sense?

Task | Look at the following sentences. When used in a particular context their meaning lies in their social function, rather than in the sense of the words. Give a context for each sentence in which it performs a social function, rather than conveying a sense.

a. *How do you do?*

b. *Lovely weather we're having for the time of year.*

c. *Have a nice day.*

d. *See you soon. Take care.*

e. *Many happy returns of the day.*

What other conversational formulae can you think of, for example *please, good morning*?

Exploration 11 • *Conversational Function*

We can say a sentence in order to convey information, as in:

a. *The Prince Regent hated his wife.*

However, instead of using a sentence to convey information, we can use it, for example, to give a judgement, as in:

b. *I reckon he's the best sprinter in the club*

or to announce a decision, as in:

c. *I have decided to claim for the damage on my insurance*

or to state a viewpoint, as in:

d. *I am opposed to violence*

or to apologise for one's behaviour, as in:

e. *I'm sorry I'm late.*

Task Look at the following sentences. Decide whether each one is being used to convey information. If that is not the case, what kind of conversational function is it performing? Is it being used, for example, for apologising, for arguing, for promising, etc.? If you consider that a sentence is being used to convey information, is it possible that it could be used for a different conversational function, given a particular context? If you came to the conclusion that a sentence is not being used to convey information, was that conclusion based on the wording of the sentence or is the conversational function only implicit? Are there any ambiguous cases in your mind?

a. *Are you quite sure we can't help?*

b. *Congratulations on your wedding anniversary!*

c. *I am going to vote for Hayes.*

d. *He said he was going to vote for Hayes.*

e. *Vote for Hayes.*

f. *We have made our engagement official.*

g. *I assume you know what you are talking about.*

h. *Please accept my deepest sympathy on your sad loss.*

i. *I am going to Portugal in the autumn.*

j. *Where on earth do you think you're going to at this time of night?*

·Task Look at the following exchanges of conversation and consider what they reveal about the underlying relationship between the two people. On what clues in the language use do you base your judgement in each case:

a. Interviewer: *Why did you buy a farm in Portugal?*

Victor Borge: *Somebody had to buy a farm in Portugal.*

b. – *I have an idea I owe you some money.*

– *You do, Mr Basil. Twelve pound ten.*

– *As much as that? Time I paid it back.*

– *It is.*

– *I will, Benson.*

– *I hope so, sir, I'm sure.*

Source: *Put Out More Flags*, Evelyn Waugh

c. Interviewer: *Do you want the job?*

Politician: *I've absolutely no ambition in that direction.*

Interviewer: *That means you do.*

Further Exploration

Collect striking examples from your own experience of the kind of language uses outlined in this chapter.

Further Reading

How to do Things with Words, J. L. Austin, Oxford University Press, 1962.

A University Grammar of English, Randolph Quirk and Sidney Greenbaum, Longman, 1973.

A University Grammar of English Workbook, R. A. Close, Longman, 1974.

18 *Language and Usage*

Here we bring all of our language skills to bear on an examination of
language in use. We look at different styles of language. What makes one
sentence formal and another informal? How do we recognise a piece of
American English or Indian English, for example?

Exploration 1 • *Word Association*

One word can bring another word to mind because they often occur in
association with one another. We can guess what the final word is likely to be
in

She bit it with her false . . .

because *teeth* is associated by frequent occurrence with *bite* and *false*.

Task | Look at the following groups of words and identify the area of
association between them. What does each of the words mean?

    a. *tack, luff, gybe,*

    b. *ampersand, pica, upper case,*

    c. *pipette, filter, solution,*

    d. *earth, flex, live,*

    e. *fetlock, martingale, hands,*

    f. *beat, pulse, rhythm,*

    g. *gazebo, ha-ha, folly,*

    h. *pretty, handsome, attractive.*

Some of the words in these groups are linked because they are used in the
same area of activity. For example *hoe, fork* and *compost* are all terms you are
likely to come across when gardening.

Other groups are made up of words that are similar in sense, as in *shocking,
disgusting, revolting.*

Task Look at the following pairs of words which are similar in sense, and state whether you would make any distinction in the way you used them, either in the kind of words you would link them with or in any other way.

a. *error/fault*
b. *avoidance/evasion*
c. *to mount/to get on*
d. *post/mail*
e. *rancid/addled*
f. *fast/quickly*

Task The writers of the Smurf cartoons insert *smurf* in the dialogue regularly in place of a word.

Look at the following sentences where the same device has been used. State the word that you consider has been replaced. How predictable do you feel it is in the context? Have you been guided to the choice of a particular word by the fact that it is part of a set idiom?

a. *He ran away as fast as his smurfs could carry him.*
b. *I shall leave no smurf unturned until I find it.*
c. *They decided to smurf their living room.*
d. *Are you feeling smurf today?*
e. *Merry Christmas and a Happy New Smurf.*
f. *She parked the smurf.*

Exploration 2 • *Connotations*

A sergeant of the Parachute Regiment pointed out to a reporter in a recent television series on the Regiment: 'Paras do not retreat. They *withdraw*.' The Oxford English Dictionary gives 'to withdraw, retire, draw back' as definitions of *retreat*. The reason the sergeant rejected the word was not because of its lexical meaning, but because of its overtone, or connotation, of defeat, which he did not think *withdraw* possessed.

A word's connotations can change with time. They can vary from group to group and from person to person.

Task What connotations do the following words possess for you? Are those connotations widely held?

a. *policeman*
b. *caviar*
c. *cigarette smoking*
d. *pigs*
e. *rock music*
f. *package holiday*
g. *comprehensive education*
h. *transport café*
i. *nuclear power*
j. *cricket*

Exploration 3 • *Emotive Connotation*

Each of the words underlined in the sentences below conveys a sense, but we can assume that an overtone of approval or disapproval is also conveyed at the same time.

Task | Give a synonym in each case that conveys the same sense without that overtone.

  a. He *smashed* the record.
  b. The place is a *slum*.
  c. I managed to *drag* him away.
  d. That was a *plucky* performance.
  e. They *gabbled* away about it.
  f. I received a *scrawl* on a bit of paper.
  g. I saw her *slink* into the house.

Task | In some cases a word can be used for the sake of its approving/disapproving overtone, rather than for its sense. You may, in fact, have felt that about some of the underlined words in the sentences above.
  Look at the following list of words. Give the sense of each one and, when used for its overtone, decide whether it conveys approval or disapproval. How distinct is the lexical sense from the connotation?

divine, obscene, fascist, awful, magic, great, racist, bloody, abysmal, dreadful.

Exploration 4 • *Reflected Meaning*

A new sense or overtone can be given to a word by the nature of the context in which it is found.

Task | Identify a word in each of the following sentences that has taken on such a reflected meaning. State its usual sense/overtone and compare it with the use in this context.

  a. The woman had been severely bruised in the attack and one of her ribs had been broken. She had, however, not been *touched*.
  b. His captors persuaded him to talk after a little *coercion*.

Exploration 5 • *Levels of Formality*

Our use of language will vary according to our relationship with the people being addressed by us. This kind of language variation is often measured by means of a five-point scale which ranges through

frozen-formal,
semi-formal,
straightforward-normal,
colloquial-familiar, and
slang

as for example in the case of

'horseless carriage/motor vehicle/car/motor/wheels or banger'.

Task | Look at the following list of words. Assume that each one belongs to the straightforward-normal style of use. Give variants for each word that would, in your opinion, be used at the frozen-formal, semi-formal, colloquial-familiar and slang levels.

to throw, policeman, to steal, to walk, the big city, father, unintelligent, a young woman, luck, to eat.

How difficult was it to find variants for any of these words at any of these levels?

Exploration 6 • *Style of Address*

Our use of language will vary according to our role in the exchange. Consider the following:

Task | A policeman returns to his panda car to find that it has been stolen. What do you consider the policeman's words are likely to be when explaining the loss to the following:
   – the policeman's fellow officer on the panda patrol,
   – a young boy asking too many tiresome questions,
   – an old lady whose telephone he wants to use to report the theft,
   – a crowd of onlookers that has gathered,
   – his station sergeant on the telephone, when reporting the theft,
   – his wife when he gets home,
   – his fellow officers off duty in the bar the day afterwards,
   – his superior officer when he is summoned before him for reprimand,
   – the judge in court at the culprit's trial.

Categorise each of the utterances you have produced for the contexts above according to its level of formality.

Task State how you would apologise for being late in the following circumstances. Add an explanation to your apology.

- for a game with some friends,
- for a meal that your mother prepared two hours earlier,
- for an appointment with the doctor,
- for tea with an aged aunt from whom you hope to inherit something,
- for a rendezvous with a boy/girl friend,
- for a rendezvous with your wife/husband who is normally late for her/his appointments,
- for an interview for a job which you dearly want to get,
- for a concert at the local leisure centre with a friend who was recently so late meeting you at the airport that you both missed the aeroplane for your holiday together. The concert has already started.
- for an appointment with your bank manager from whom you want a loan,
- for a reception by the mayor of the town for the team of which you are captain and which has just won a national championship.

Categorise each apology according to its level of formality.

Exploration 7 • *Register*

Our use of language will vary according to the activity in which we are currently involved.

Task Look at the following extracts, the sources of which are stated in brackets below, and identify examples of choice of words and structural arrangement which, in your opinion, are typical of the language use of that area of activity.

State also the extent to which the level of formality of the language is important for the appropriateness of each extract in its context.

a. *West Ham Match Switch Idea Rejected* (headline in *The Times*)

b. *No ifs. No buts. No surcharges.* (travel firm's advertisement)

c. *This brings the best of good wishes to you for good luck and success in all that you do.* (message on a greetings card)

d. *With honesty of intent I have made all these offerings gladly, and gladly have I seen all that are here assembled.* (prayer at a communion service)

e. *All members of the Licensee's family and domestic staff while in residence in the said premises (otherwise than in a part thereof which is not in the occupation of the Licensee) and all members of the Licensee's family so resident while living elsewhere for the purpose of receiving a full-time course of education at an educational establishment are hereby licensed . . .* (television licence)

Task Look at the following extracts and state the profession or area of activity in which the speaker/writer is engaged, in your opinion. What words and structural arrangements have led you to your choice? To what extent does the level of formality contribute to the overall impression conveyed by each extract?

a. *A switch on the control satellite alters the fuel range display to read distance travelled, average speed, fuel consumption since resetting, or exterior temperature. Economy is good for a lively 1.7 litre. The 11 TXE gave 28 mpg overall, but easily topped 35 mpg when cruising moderately fast on a long journey.*

b. *The uncertainty soon prompted a markdown, but there was no great weight of selling. However, in the context few investors were willing to chance their arm, so it was left to the share tips and special situation stocks to monopolise most of the business.*

c. *Where the burden lies on the executive to justify the exercise of a power of detention, the facts relied on as justification must be proved to the satisfaction of the court. A preponderance of probability must be such that the court is satisfied.*

Task Look at the following extracts of spoken or written English. Give a probable context of use for each one. What words and structural arrangements have led you to your choice? What is the attitude of the writer to the subject matter?

a. *In summer the earth leans towards the sun, so that we can bask in its heat and have long, sunny days. In between these two extremes of cold and heat, we have the seasons of spring and autumn when it is neither very cold nor very hot.*

b. *There were no nuclear holocausts in Scotland today. This brings Scotland into line with the rest of the world.*

c. *If you enjoy mingling with the stars, then you're in luck. On Tuesday 9 March, after the performance of the hilarious comedy FUR COAT AND NO KNICKERS we'll be holding a 'Meet the Cast Evening' in the Lower Foyer. Liz Fraser, who must be one of this country's most popular actresses – remember her in the 'Carry On' films? – heads an all-star cast which includes Ivan Beavis and Lawrence Mullin (best known for their appearances as Harry Hewitt and Steve Fisher in 'Coronation Street').*

Exploration 8 • *Regional Variation*

Our use of language can vary according to the geographical region from which we come.

In 6 Exploration 2 we looked at differences in pronunciation between RP and the accent termed General American or Network American. In 7 Exploration 2 we considered different stress patterns given to the same words by British and American English pronunciations. Let us now look at differences of words and structure between standard British and American English usage.

Task If an American English speaker uses the following terms, what words is a British English speaker more likely to use in their stead?

gasoline, windshield, elevator, janitor, thumb tack, trashcan, cream pitcher, clothes pins, intermission, (the) drapes, faucet, mortician, (car) trunk, realtor, (car) muffler, a (salary) raise, billboard, (to) mail, cookie, sedan.

How many of these words are already familiar to you in their American English use? How many would you use in preference to their British English equivalent?

Task The following American English terms have been adopted by speakers of British English in preference to the original British usage. State the original British terms they have superseded or are in the process of superseding.

teenager, blizzard, rare (steak), allergy, billion, sneakers, camper (vehicle), corn (as in cornflakes), a cook-book, movie.

Task Look at the sentences below and identify any features in them which, while understanding them, you would consider to be more typical of an American English speaker than of a British English one.

a. *I keep thinking of them driving around nights.*
b. *Mary's gotten herself a new car.*
c. *The office is open Monday thru Friday.*
d. *Did you finish your dinner already?*
e. *They always write me at Christmas.*
f. *Boy, she can really sleep some.*
g. *They wanted that I go.*
h. *Do you want to hold the door for me?* (as a request for help)
i. *Her report was different than the real event.*
j. *Somebody dove into the water to save her.*

139

Further Explorations

Examine other regional dialect variations from standard British usage.

Examine register, levels of formality and connotation in different kinds of English usage, e.g. advertising, political speeches.

Further Reading

Variety in Contemporary English, W. R. O'Donnell and Loreto Todd, George Allen & Unwin, 1980.

On Dialect, Peter Trudgill, Blackwell, 1983.

International English, Peter Trudgill and Jean Hannah, Edward Arnold, 1982.

Problems in the Origins and Development of the English Language, John Algeo, Harcourt Brace Jovanovich, 1966.

19 *Language Change*

We end this journey through language by looking at some of the ways in which language changes over time. How do these changes – in sound, meaning and use – come about? Should we strive to protect the language from change? Can we in fact do so?

Exploration 1 • *Sound Change*

A language is in a constant state of change. An older British English speaker is more likely to have learned to call the object a

a. *wireless* than a

b. *radio*

and is more likely to say

a. *I haven't seen her for three days* than

b. *I haven't seen her in three days*.

In 6 Exploration 1 we saw that change was taking place in the RP pronunciation of the diphthong [ʊə]. It is being replaced by the vowel [ɔː] in the pronunciation of *tour*, for example, by many RP speakers.

One of the most celebrated changes in English pronunciation over the centuries is known as the Great Vowel Shift. It involved the long vowels of Middle English:

1. [iː]   2. [eː]   3. [ɛː]   4. [aː]   5. [uː]   6. [oː]   7. [ɔː]

Gradually, between the 14th and the early 18th century, the pronunciation of these sounds changed and their most frequent equivalents in RP English now are:

1. [aɪ]   2. [iː]   3. [eɪ]   4. [eɪ]   5. [aʊ]   6. [uː]   7. [əʊ]

The corresponding short vowels in Middle English did not go through a similar change, however. As a result modern English contains pairs such as (original long vowel first):

ride/ridden, leave/left, sane/sanity, house/husband, goose/gosling, go/gone.

Task | Look at the following words with vowels derived from long vowels of Middle English and, following the pattern of these related pairs above, give a cognate word with a vowel derived from a comparable Middle English short vowel.

to read, lively, sleep, late, break, holy, choose, shoe, child, case, please, wide, out, wife, do, thief, five, deep, hide, lose.

Exploration 2 • *Borrowings*

In 8 Explorations 2, 3, 7 and 8 we saw how words can be created by the addition of affixes to existing words.

In 8 Exploration 9 we saw how new words can be created by the removal of what is mistakenly supposed to be an affix – backformation.

A language can also acquire new words by adopting words from other languages.

Task | Look at the following words of English. They have all been borrowed from another language. With the help of the large *Oxford English Dictionary* or any other etymological dictionary discover the language from which they were taken, as well as their meaning in that language.

check-mate, whisky, baroque, propaganda, jubilee, robot, zero, typhoon, bungalow, gong.

Exploration 3 • *Blends*

New words can be created in English by running together two existing words. An example of such a blend is *stuffocate* from *stifle* and *suffocate* or *brunch* from *breakfast* and *lunch*.

Task | Of which English words are the following a blend?

smog, motel, subtopia, transistor, newscaster, motorcade, biopic, galumph, flurry, Amerindian.

Exploration 4 • *Acronyms*

Acronyms are words composed of the initial letters of other words. The names of many modern pressure groups are acronyms of words that describe their purpose, for example ASH is *Action on Smoking and Health*, an anti-tobacco group.

Task | Look at the following acronyms and state the words that lie behind them.

flak, laser, radar, bren (gun), ufo, sonar, quango.

Exploration 5 • *Shortening of Words*

A new word can be created by shortening an existing one to the syllable carrying the principle stress. For example, *bicycle* is shortened to *bike* and *microphone* to *mike*.

Task | Look at the following words and state the longer words of which they were originally a shortening.

pram, (a) fence, wig, perk, disco, flu, tend, nark, size, car.

In which cases has the initial syllable been dropped? In which cases have final syllables been dropped?

Exploration 6 • *Expansion and Contraction of Sense*

The sense of a word can be broadened. For example *bird* originally referred to a young bird only.

The sense of a word can become more narrow. For example *meat* originally referred to any kind of food, not just animal flesh.

Task | Look at the following words which have either expanded or contracted their earlier senses. State what those earlier senses were and whether there is any survival of them in present-day English, e.g. as the earlier sense of *meat* survives in *sweetmeat*.

fowl, science, undertaker, deer, hound, starve, wealth, counterfeit, doctor, tabloid.

Exploration 7 • *Complete Change of Sense*

Words can change their sense completely. For example, the word *presently* in Shakespearean English meant *at once, at the present time*. Then it came to mean *in the near future*, although it is in fact beginning to be used in the earlier sense again, as it is in American English.

Task | Look at the following words that have undergone a change of sense and state what that sense originally was.

silly, posy, sensible, tide, fond, wit, nice, quaint, journey, bead.

State whether examples of the earlier uses can still be found in present-day English, e.g. *a nice distinction* meaning a 'fine' or 'detailed' one.

Exploration 8 • *Words Fallen out of Use*

Words can fall out of use.

Task | What was the meaning of the following words, which have fallen out of common use?

wot, welkin, fain, bant, filfot, mizzle, cordwainer, bobbysoxer, (a) lucifer, spiffing.

Did you recognise any of these words and, if so, are there any circumstances in which you are likely to use them? Can you envisage any circumstance in which they could come into common use again, as has been the case with *carrel, probe* and *capsule.*

Exploration 9 • *Eponyms*

New words can be created, based on a person's name. They can embody the qualities that made the original famous. People's names are often used to form words to convey objects, ideas, etc. with which they are associated. For example *wellingtons* are named after the first Duke of Wellington and *boycott* after the nineteenth century Captain Charles Boycott, who was ostracised for his behaviour as an Irish land agent.

Task | Look at the following words, based on the names of people, give their meanings and state the circumstances that gave rise to them.

tawdry, grangerise, dahlia, draconian, greengage, tarmac, leotard, pinchbeck, pasteurise, chauvinist.

Can you think of words of English that are derived from place names, e.g. *rugby*?

Exploration 10 • *Changes in Structure*

Change in structure takes place more slowly than change amongst the word stock of a language.

Task | Look at the following examples of English from the age of Shakespeare and the Authorised Version of the Bible. Each sentence contains a structural element which, though recognisable to modern English speakers, is unlikely to be used by them in everyday circumstances.

It is characteristic of certain registers of English, for example legal, religious and ceremonial usage, that they retain words and structures that are not commonly found in modern usage.

> Identify in these sentences structural devices that have fallen out of everyday use and, if they are already familiar to you, state the language context in which you would have expected to find them.
>
> a. *I am just come out of the garden.*
> b. *Methinks the lady doth protest too much.*
> c. *She loves me; she loves me not.*
> d. *Wherefore I do entreat you to hear me.*
>   (not an emphatic use of 'do')
> e. *Our Father who art in heaven . . .*
> f. *The explosion blow'd the weather boarding off.*
> g. *Help me or I sink.*
> h. *Thy mother and thy sister seek thee.*

Further Exploration

Collect for your *Data Book* further examples of language change.

Read up the history of the development of English and examine in detail some particular aspect of it, e.g. Shakespearean or 18th-century English usage.

Further Reading

A History of the English Language, Albert C. Baugh and Thomas Cable, Routledge & Kegan Paul, Third Edition, 1978.

The Origins and Development of the English Language, Thomas Pyles, Harcourt Brace Jovanovich, 1964.

Problems in the Origins and Development of the English Language, John Algeo, Harcourt Brace Jovanovich, 1966.

The Making of English, Henry Bradley, Macmillan, reissued 1968.